Borders by Design

CREATIVE WAYS TO BORDER YOUR QUILTS

That Patchwork Place®

Paulette Peters

Credits

Editor-in-Chief . . . . Barbara Weiland
Technical Editor . . . . Janet White
Managing Editor . . . . Greg Sharp
Copy Editor . . . . Tina Cook
Proofreader . . . . Leslie Phillips
Text and Cover Designer . . . . David Chrisman
Photographer . . . . Brent Kane
Illustrator . . . . Brian Metz

Borders by Design: Creative Ways to Border Your Quilts
© 1994 by Paulette Peters
That Patchwork Place, Inc.
PO Box 118
Bothell, WA 98041-0118 USA

Printed in the United States of America
03 02 01 00 99 98   13 12 11 10 9 8

Library of Congress Cataloging-in-Publication Data
Peters, Paulette
    Borders by design : creative ways to border your quilts / Paulette Peters.
        p.   cm.
    Includes bibliographical references.
    ISBN 1-56477-082-6 :
    1. Quilts. 2. Borders, Ornamental (Decorative arts) I. Title.
TT835.P4492 1994
746.46—dc20   94-36946
                                                        CIP

Acknowledgments

I am grateful to:

The anonymous quilt mothers, who inspire our generation's quilting sensibilities.

The teachers and quilt leaders of our time, who have been my special inspirations: Jinny Beyer, Marianne Fons, and Mary Ellen Hopkins, for classes and books; Mary Jo Dalrymple, for challenging me to think and look; Lois Gottsch, for years of "Quilt Talk"; Mary Hickey, Nancy J. Martin, and Marsha McCloskey, for personal and professional encouragement.

Barbara Weiland, for trusting that I would bring her idea to publication, and Janet White, for helping me do that.

Dedication

For Leslie, Mike, and Gregg, who seem to believe that their mother is as capable as they are. And for Terry, most of all.

Contents

INTRODUCTION

There are no rules about quilt borders, but there are many questions. How wide should my borders be? How narrow? Should they be pieced, appliquéd, or plain? What's the best way to frame the quilt? How much quilting do I want to do? How can I make this quilt big enough for the bed when I'm tired of piecing? There are many answers to these questions. Only you can decide what your rules will be for a particular quilt.

Borders are the hidden factor in creating a pleasing quilt. If the quilt seems a little bit "off," look at the border. It may be out of proportion. If the quilt is beautifully framed and attention focuses on the center, look at the border. It is doing its duty.

A truly beautiful border can be as simple as plain pieces of fabric or as complicated as many tiny blocks sewn together into strips. If it enhances the quilt without distraction, if it is well integrated into the design, it is a beautiful border.

This is not a pattern book. It is a resource for designing your own borders. *Borders by Design* introduces you to three principles of border design: Divide the Side, Use the Unit, and Connect the Corner. The book describes techniques that help you avoid some of the common border-construction pitfalls and gives specific directions to get you started on designing the perfect border for any quilt. I hope *Borders by Design* inspires you to really enjoy "working on the edge!"

HISTORY

As in any area of quiltmaking, borders offer the opportunity to take traditional techniques and adapt them for modern quiltmaking. Many historical quilts display expanses of beautiful printed chintz or flowered fabric on wide, straight borders. If a quiltmaker had access to yard goods and could afford a long piece, she featured it at the edge of the quilt and coordinated the main part of the quilt with that piece of fabric. Fairly "active" and large-scale prints made the quilting design less visible and less important.

Early Amish quilts also have wide borders. The plain fabrics perfectly display the lovely quilting designs that enhance the quilt surfaces. If quilting is the process you love, consider a plain fabric border, which offers you a space to show off.

Some of the charm and quirkiness of old quilts come from unconcern for matched corners. Quiltmakers often made four pieced strips exactly alike and attached them to the quilt.

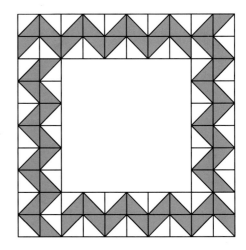

This unconcern sometimes resulted in a quilt with two similar corners and two corners with different arrangements, or four random corners.

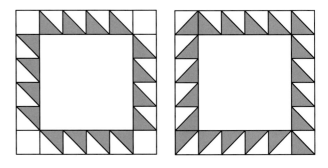

Occasionally, a quiltmaker made a pieced strip, attached it to the quilt, and simply cut it off at the edge.

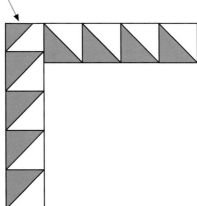

If you are reproducing an old quilt, working with scraps, or trying to achieve an antique look, these techniques can add spontaneity to your piece.

Like most of today's quilts, many of the appliquéd borders and some of the pieced borders of the past were carefully planned so that all four corners were the same and the design flowed around the border without a break. These borders exhibit the symmetry and rhythm that result from matched corners and careful spacing of design units.

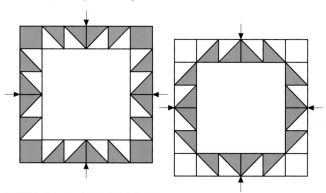

WHY ADD A BORDER?

Some reasons for adding borders include:

❖ **Framing the quilt.** Like a painting, a quilt design may need a transition from the focal point to the edge. A wall quilt may need a buffer between the pattern and the wall where it will hang, so that the design area predominates. A bed quilt may need a mattress drop, so that the focal area is centered on the bed top. The design may simply need something to make the center of the quilt sparkle or calm down.

❖ **Adjusting the size of the quilt.** What if the quilt is too small for the intended use and adding another block to each side would make it too large? Aha! Add a border!

❖ **Stopping the design.** The quilt design keeps moving out from the center, with lots of motion and activity, and the edges just keep going. Patterns such as tumbling blocks or pyramids, or any of the tessellated patterns, could grow to take over the world without borders to contain them!

❖ **Continuing the design.** Perhaps your central design seems unfinished. Complete an important design element by extending just one part of it into the border. Use this technique to transform traditional blocks into a contemporary-feeling quilt. (See "Ribbon Star with asymmetrical borders," page 33.)

❖ **Showing off.** Borders provide excellent areas to display your appliqué ability, your piecing perfection, or your quilting quality.

RIBBON STAR BLOCKS

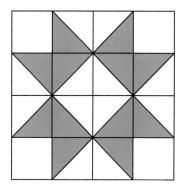

This familiar quilt block has many names. It's fun because it is such a chameleon, adaptable to many moods and possibilities. Some of the photographed and illustrated quilts in this book use Ribbon Star blocks in the quilt center.

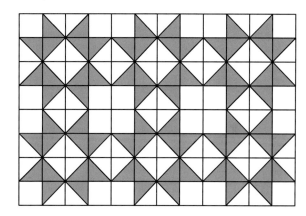

Borders change the mood of a quilt and complete it. In the Ribbon Star Series quilts in the Gallery, I used six blocks, set together without sashing. They looked fine alone—until borders were added. Then the six blocks looked so much more finished. Carefully examine the photographs of the Ribbon Star quilts, pages 32–34, to see the different visual effects you can create with different border styles.

Directions for an 8" and a 12" Ribbon Star block are on page 58.

Design Principles

The most important consideration in designing a good border is unity. The border should relate to the quilt as a whole. Some aspects of unity include: rhythm, flow, balance, and proportion. If you understand these principles, you will find it easier to design effective borders for your quilts.

RHYTHM

Rhythm is accomplished through the repetition of a design element. Achieve visual rhythm by using the same fabric, color, or block design in both the center and border of the quilt.

FLOW

Flow describes unbroken movement within a design. Does the quilt make a smooth transition from the focal point to the edge? To make a successful transition, use appropriate border widths, blend colors from the quilt center to the edges, or extend the central design elements into the border. Make the border look as if it belongs on that quilt and wasn't added as an afterthought.

Multiple borders create additional considerations. The various borders should be compatible with each other in color, size, and pattern. Well-designed multiple borders flow from the center to the outside of the quilt without making the eye jump from center to edge and border to border.

A border that ends too abruptly draws the eye to that spot. (See "Interior Borders," page 40.) If the border cuts off part of the quilt, add a piece to the border that will finish the design.

Do the corners of each border connect and relate well to the rest of the border? Quiltmakers often treat corners as units separate from the rest of the border, but they should have some relationship with it, so that the design flows around the quilt without interruption.

BALANCE

Balance describes a pattern in which no one element outweighs or detracts from another. Balance can be achieved in many ways. Are there curves in the quilt design? Sometimes the border needs to repeat the curves, and sometimes it needs angles to balance all those curves. Likewise, a very angular, geometric quilt might need the balance of some curves in its border.

(See "Edgewise," page 29.)

Appliquéd borders often enhance a pieced quilt and appliquéd quilts often have pieced borders. Although the techniques are different, design unity can be maintained. Choose a pieced design that repeats one of the curves in the appliqué, or extend the appliqué into the pieced areas. (See "Through the Trellis Garden Again," page 32.)

Are there intense colors in the design? You may want to repeat those colors in smaller amounts in the border, or you might make the border a "resting place" for the eye, to balance the excitement in the center and focus attention on it.

PROPORTION

Proportion refers to a pleasing relation of parts within a whole. Play with the size of various design elements to achieve proportion in your quilt.

To maintain emphasis at the center of the quilt, use pattern pieces of the same size in the border and quilt center, or use smaller pieces in the border. For example, if the blocks use 3" pieces, the pieced border could also use 3" pieces. Or, make the border pieces even smaller, using 1½" pieces. If the blocks use 4" pieces, the pieced border could also use 4" pieces, or smaller, 2" pieces.

You can use a larger scale for the borders if the quilt is very active and needs a calmer place for the eye. However, a larger-scale border often just looks as if you were tired of piecing.

Make sure your borders are in good proportion to the quilt center. A border that is too narrow makes the quilt look unfinished. A border that is too wide looks heavy and overwhelms the center.

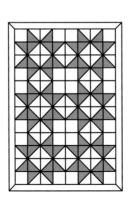
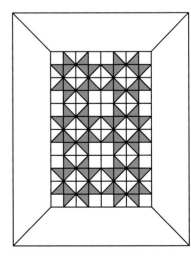

As a rule, relate border width to some element of the piecing in the quilt design. For example, your quilt may use 12" blocks. Twelve inches divide easily by 2", 3", 4", and 6". Use one or more of these measurements in your border piecing. Combinations of several widths are usually more pleasing than one large expanse.

Possible Border Widths for 12-inch Blocks

Half the Block Size (6")

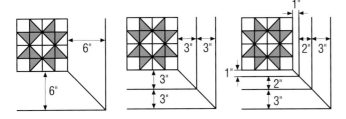

Three-Fourths of the Block Size (9")

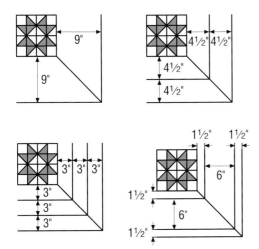

If possible, make the border no wider than three-fourths of the block size. The exception would be when using a block from the quilt as a corner square (see "Ribbon Star, straight borders with quilt block corners," page 34) or when adding an elaborate appliqué border.

TIP: 1-2-3 Border

For a pleasing border arrangement, graduate the border widths from narrowest to widest. The basic unit is the inner border. Double it for the middle border and triple it for the outer border. For example: 1", 2", and 3"; 1½", 3", and 4½"; and 2", 4", and 6".

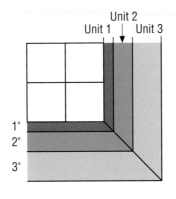

Design Methods

LOOK, LOOK, LOOK—at quilts, paintings, architecture, printed material—anything with a border or an interesting edge. Think about what you're seeing. Why does that border look skimpy? Why is that one too heavy? Discover what you like. Then apply your personal taste to your quilt.

On a practical level, you can plan the border when you plan the quilt, but often the quilt tells you what it wants after the center blocks are finished. I like the flexibility of waiting until the top is pieced before I plan the borders.

It is a good idea to audition border designs before beginning to sew. As you look at your ideas, keep in mind your purpose, the elements of unity, and what appeals to you. Remember the goal: Unity in rhythm, flow, balance and proportion. Look for the "Golden Mean"—the balance of perfect harmony. This is the fun part. Play with it.

Graph Paper

Use graph paper to make a scale drawing of a corner or all of the quilt center. Make several photocopies of this drawing and cut your design out. Paste the copies on new sheets of graph paper and experiment by drawing borders around them.

Graph paper makes it easy to draw designs to scale, helping you to visualize your pattern. It's easier to draw your borders if you know the unit size.

1. Find the unit size for your border. (See page 20.)
2. Assign a size to each little square on the graph paper. If the unit size is 3", pretend that each square on the graph paper is 1". This is your scale: 1 square = 1". Now make a dot every 3 squares. This will be one unit in your border.

   If the unit size is a fraction, like 3½", make each square equal ½". Scale: 1 square = ½". Make a dot every 7 squares. This will be one unit in your border.
3. When your drawing is complete and you are ready to cut fabric, count the squares and multiply them by your scale size to determine what size each piece will be.
4. Add seam allowances before cutting pieces from fabric.

Transparencies

Another method is to make a copy of the quilt center on a transparency like those used in overhead projectors. On graph paper, draw only the outline of the quilt center. Experiment by drawing several border choices around the outlined center, and then overlay the quilt center transparency on these drawings to see how the patterns interact.

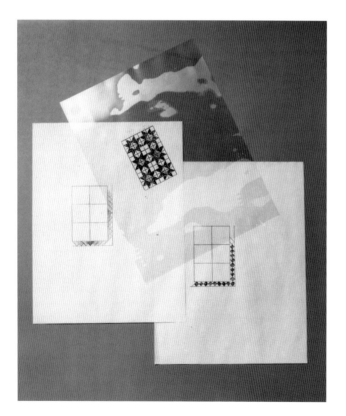

Fabric Paste-Up

Fabric paste-up is really fun. Be careful that you don't get so caught up in pasting little quilt borders that you forget to make the real one!
1. Draw a corner of the quilt pattern on graph paper.
2. Apply spray adhesive to several pieces of good-quality tracing paper, following the manufacturer's directions. (See "Tools," page 9.)
3. Tape a piece of tracing paper over the line drawing. Cut small pieces of fabric in the shapes required to create your border design and stick them down. You may need a pair of tweezers.
4. Using your graph-paper quilt pattern, repeat this tracing-paper paste-up technique as many times as you like.

Design Wall

A design wall is a wonderful tool. I can't imagine getting along without one. Use a piece of flannel or batting hung on a wall or attached to a large sheet (4' x 8') of Styrofoam insulation.

If the center of the quilt is finished, hang it up on the design wall and audition various fabrics for possible borders. Pin a strip of fabric across the top, fold a mitered corner, and allow the rest of the fabric strip to hang down along the side. Now step back at least five feet and consider. Replace and rearrange the border fabrics until you are satisfied. This is a wonderful way to visualize your finished quilt without committing yourself with needle and thread.

TOOLS

These tools will help you create and apply borders.

Work Surface. A large cutting and measuring surface is great for laying large pieces of fabric out flat. If possible, make yours a height that is comfortable for you when standing. Some quilters use sawhorses and a large sheet of plywood. Some use a work table, the kitchen counter, or the dining room table. Agile quilters use the floor.

Tape Measure. Attach a tape measure to your tabletop. Look for an adhesive-backed tape measure in the notions department of your favorite fabric store. This can be permanently applied to the edge of the table. If dinner must be served on this table occasionally, simply fasten a soft tape measure to the table with transparent tape instead.

Rotary Cutter and Mat. The larger the mat, the better. A mat with a grid is helpful for keeping long lengths of fabric straight and for measuring accurately. A smaller mat also works; just slip it under the fabric at the point where you want to cut.

Long Rotary Ruler. Use for cutting lengths of fabric across the grain or along the length of the grain.

Bias Square® or 45° Drafting Triangle. Use for measuring and cutting mitered corners.

Long Metal Tape Measure. Retractable tape measures used by carpenters make measuring the quilt top so much easier, especially if you have another person to hold down one side.

Masking Tape. Use to tape one end of a border piece to the table so that you can measure and cut at the other end.

Ruler. Purchase a 2"-wide, clear acrylic ruler, marked in ⅛" grids. Use this for drawing on paper, not for cutting with a rotary cutter.

Graph Paper. Purchase graph paper with eight squares to the inch. Use it to sketch border ideas and draw borders to scale. If you like a larger drawing, use the large sheets, four squares to the inch, found in desk pads.

Tracing Paper. You will need good-quality tracing paper, in a size to match your graph paper. (See "Fabric Paste-Up," page 8.)

Calculator. Use a calculator to make quick work of the simple math necessary to design borders.

Sharp Pencil. Mechanical pencils with fine lead work well for drawing on paper and for marking light fabrics.

Spray Adhesive. Be sure that the directions say "repositionable" so you can move fabric around. Follow the manufacturer's safety precautions. (See "Fabric Paste-Up," page 8.)

Glue Stick. These are available with adhesive that can be repositioned. You can use them instead of spray adhesive for paste-up designing.

Transparencies. Use transparencies to design borders and audition them with your quilt-top drawing. (See "Transparencies," page 8.)

Adding-Machine Paper Rolls. Buy the widest you can find, usually 3" wide. Use to fold pattern segments when designing appliquéd or pieced borders. (See "Appliqué Borders," page 48.)

Iron. I use a dry iron because steam tends to "spit" at the wrong moment. If the fabric needs to be tamed, use spray sizing rather than steam.

Ironing Board Cover. Look for one that is as flat and "non-puffy" as it can be without allowing your board to burn. I like a cover with a printed grid. You can make your own grid by drawing a straight line on the cover with a permanent pen. Draw another line at a 90° angle and heat set it. Check the cover periodically with a ruler to make sure the lines are not distorted.

Pressing Mat. Sometimes you need to press a part of your border without moving it from the large cutting surface. Slip a handy portable pressing mat under the quilt top to press a small area.

Pins. In normal piecing I do a minimum of pinning, but pins are helpful when adding borders. It is easy to find the glass head of a long quilter's pin in masses of fabric. I use safety pins to mark the halfway point and the quarter mark of each quilt edge and border. They are easy to find, and they don't fall out.

Seam Guide. Many sewing machines include seam guides. They reduce wobbling and improve accuracy in the long seams that join quilt tops and borders.

Extra Finger. To help guide fabric into the sewing machine without stitching your fingers, try a long, pointy tweezers; a seam ripper; or a pencil with no lead.

TECHNIQUES

The techniques that follow are specifically for cutting and applying borders. It is not within the scope of this book to give extensive information on basic quilt cutting and piecing techniques. You can find helpful information on these subjects in *The Quilters' Companion* or the individual Joy of Quilting books, published by That Patchwork Place.

Measuring Your Quilt Top for Borders

Use a metal, retractable tape measure to find the length and width through the middle of the quilt. These will be your cutting lengths.

Always cut the borders to the correct size, and make the quilt top fit the border. Simply cutting a long strip, sewing it to the quilt, and trimming the excess length results in wavy edges, unsquare corners, and a quilt that is longer on one side than the other. If one side of the quilt is slightly longer than the other, the time to correct it is before the border is applied.

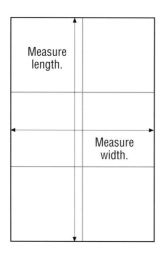

Cut both side borders the same length, and make the top fit them by easing or gently stretching the top where necessary. Cut the borders for the top and bottom edges to equal the quilt's width measurement, and make the top fit them. If two sides vary in length by more than ¾", find a place to correct it in the piecing of the quilt.

TIP: Suppose you have made a quilt from a pattern, and you know how big it is supposed to be. Measure it anyway! Don't assume that your piecing is perfect.

Yardage Estimates

Borders Cut from the Lengthwise Grain

To calculate yardage for borders cut on the lengthwise grain without piecing, determine the length of the longest border plus seam allowances. Add ⅛ yard to allow for shrinkage. Remember that you need 6" extra for mitered borders.

Cut the borders first, and then use the rest of the fabric for piecing the quilt center. If you haven't planned that far, take the piecing yardage from one side of the fabric length, leaving the other side for borders.

Borders Cut on the Crosswise Grain

1. Find the total length of all borders:

   Width of quilt (including border) x 2 = _____
   + length of quilt x 2 = _____
   Total border length _____

2. How many cuts will you need?

   Total border length _____ ÷ 42" = _____
   (step 1)   (fabric   Number of cuts
               width)   (round up if
                         necessary)

3. How many inches will you need?

   Number of cuts_____ x _____ = _____
           (step 2)   Border width   Inches needed
                    (+ seam
                    allowances)

4. How many yards to buy?

   _____ ÷ 36 = _____
   Inches needed   Yards to buy

Cutting Borders

Avoid bias edges on a border! In a pieced border, cut all edge pieces on the straight grain. For plain borders, you may cut strips on the lengthwise or crosswise grain of the fabric.

If possible, cut borders on the long grain of the fabric (parallel to the selvages). This may require a little more fabric, but for stability and for preventing wavy quilt edges, it's worth it. Never use the selvages. They are tightly woven and will not give at all, which can cause unsightly pulling. Trim away selvages, and then cut border pieces along the full length of the fabric.

You may also cut borders on the crosswise grain (selvage to selvage). These will stretch a little more and need to be pinned more closely when applying them to the quilt. For large quilts, it will be necessary to piece border strips to make them long enough to fit.

To piece border strips, use a diagonal seam. It is stronger and less noticeable than a straight seam.

1. Cut the border strips, making sure that the ends are exactly square. Use your rotary cutter and ruler to square them up before piecing them together.

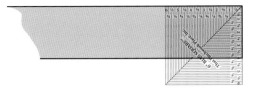

2. Place one border piece, right side up, on the table. Place another face down, aligning squared edges.

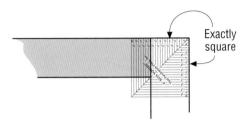

Exactly square

3. Mark an exact right angle. Pin in place, and stitch on the marked line. Press the seam open and trim excess fabric.

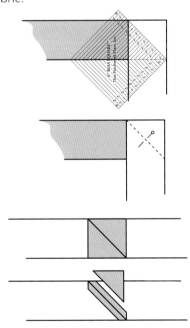

4. Place the seam in an inconspicuous spot on the border, not at the center or only a few inches from the end. Measure and cut border lengths from the pieced strip.

Always cut the two long borders together and the two short together, so that they measure exactly the same. This will make the quilt sides match exactly. Layer two border strips, which have been cut to the correct width, along the tape measure attached to the table

edge. (See "Tape Measure," page 9.) Cut an exact right angle at the end. With masking tape, tape the end of the borders at the exact spot where zero shows on the tape measure. This will prevent "creeping" of the fabric before you're ready to cut. Find the correct measurement on the tape measure, slip the cutting board under the fabric, and rotary cut the end at an exact right angle.

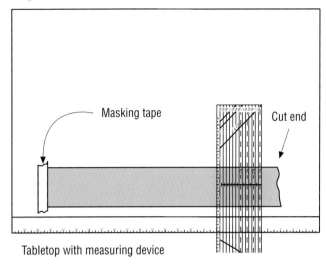

Masking tape   Cut end

Tabletop with measuring device

What if the table is too short for the length of the borders? Tape the end of the fabric at zero, measure 20", and mark it in the seam allowance. Move that mark back to zero, tape it down, and find the final measurement, minus 20", to use as a cutting line.

Adding Borders to the Quilt Top

Pin, pin, pin! Pin-basting distributes the length of the border evenly, so that any easing can be spread over the whole seam.

1. Fold the quilt in half and place a pin at the center point of the quilt edge. I like to use a safety pin, which won't slip out, and I mark the center on all four sides at the same time.
2. Find the center of one border and mark it with a pin.
3. Match the center point of the border with the center point of the quilt side and pin.

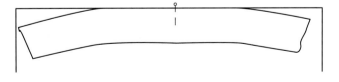

4. Match the ends and pin them.

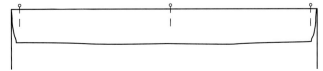

5. Now place a pin halfway between those points, and then halfway between those points. Keep dividing the spaces between pins and pinning until there is a pin every 3–4 inches.

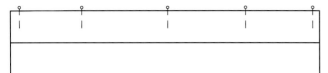

6. Set your seam guide at ¼". (Refer to "Tools," page 9.) Use the guide as a ledge to keep the fabric feeding straight into the machine. Remove the pins as you approach them with the sewing machine needle, before they tangle with the seam guide.

Is the border added to the quilt, or the quilt to the border? Whichever edge has the most piecing should be on top as you feed the fabric through the machine, so that you can see where the border seam line should cross the piecing.

For example, a sawtooth border has many triangles. Place it face down on the right side of the quilt, and stitch at the exact point where the triangles meet the seam allowance. If a plain border is added to a quilt top with lots of seams at the edge, place the quilt face down on the border so you can see the points to be matched as you stitch.

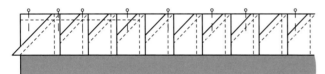

Do you need to ease one side to fit? Distribute the fullness evenly and pin very closely. Put the longer side on the bottom, face up, and the shorter side on the top, face down. Let the machine help. It pushes the top layer a little.

Lockstitching

Usually it isn't necessary to backstitch when piecing. However, in certain cases, you should secure the ends of a seam with lockstitching. Lockstitch the last seams of the last border to hold the edge of the quilt while it is handled for quilting.

Lockstitch exactly ¼" from the quilt edge when mitering corners. (Refer to "Borders with Mitered Corners," page 15.) There is more than one way to lockstitch. You can:

❖ Stitch forward two or three stitches. Backstitch two or three stitches, and then go forward again.

❖ Take several stitches in the same spot before going forward. (Set the machine stitch length at 0.)

Chain Piecing

This method saves time and thread when piecing many identical units.

1. Sew the first pair of pieces from cut edge to cut edge. At the end of the seam, stop sewing but do not cut the thread.

2. Feed the next pair of pieces under the presser foot, as close as possible to the first pair. Continue feeding pieces through the machine without cutting the threads in between. There is no need to backstitch, since each seam will be crossed and held by another seam.

3. When all pieces have been sewn, remove the chain from the machine and clip the threads between the pieces.

After completing the first chain, piece the units in pairs of two, then pairs of four, then pairs of eight, and so on. I love sewing pieced borders. They grow so fast!

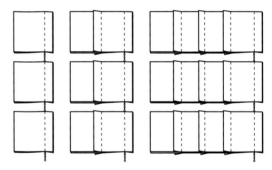

Pressing Borders

Press from the front, or top, of the border. Press carefully. Seams easily stretch and distort if you move your iron across the quilt top. Press, and then lift the iron before moving it.

While pressing, keep the border seam aligned with the ironing-board grid to keep the border straight. (Refer to "Tools," page 9.)

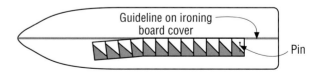

Guideline on ironing board cover

Pin

In general, press seams toward borders, away from the quilt. First, settle the stitches into the fabric by pressing over the seam you have just sewn, without opening it. Then fold the border away from the quilt and pin one end of the border to the ironing board.

Align the border edge with the marked line and press. To avoid stretching, press and lift, moving outward across the border, not along its length. Press a crisp, straight seam.

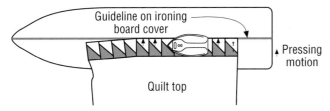

TIP: Despite careful measuring, piecing, and pressing, quilt edges occasionally flare out. If this is the case, before layering for quilting, measure the quilt width and length through the center of the quilt. Cut 1½"-wide strips equaling the width and length measurements as you would for straight-cut borders and add a strip to each side of the quilt. This controls the edge and adds only 1" to each side.

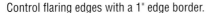

Control flaring edges with a 1" edge border.

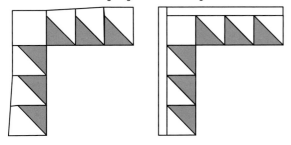

Quilting Borders

A few quilting principles apply specifically to borders. Once again, strive to unite the borders and the quilt center. Use a quilting design that complements the quilt pattern while applying the following principles:

❖ Use similar amounts of quilting for the border and for the quilt center. Close, intricate stitching in the center with less quilting in the borders results in weak, puffy borders. Close stitching in the borders with less quilting in the center causes the center to "dish" out like a saucer.

Quilt the corners as heavily as the sides and center of the quilt. These are often neglected areas and need strength to keep the quilt in shape.

❖ Straight lines of quilting, parallel to the border edges, are hard to keep straight, and any wobbling in the line is noticeable. Straight quilting lines are more vulnerable to breaking with use than patterned quilting.

To avoid problems, plan the quilting to zigzag or curve across the width of the borders. Or, quilt radiating lines at 45° or 90° angles from the body of the quilt.

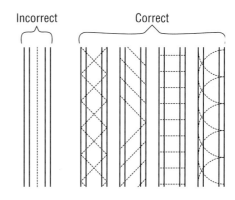

❖ To mark quilting lines, start at the center of each border. Measure the units along each side of the border and pin or mark those points before marking the quilting design. Then connect the dots with a ruler and marker. Don't rely on measuring from your last quilting line.

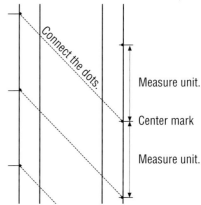

❖ Avoid stretching the edges during quilting by minimizing the tension on them. Try these methods:

Baste a strip of muslin to the edge of the quilt. Use the muslin for attaching the quilt top to a quilt frame or hoop.

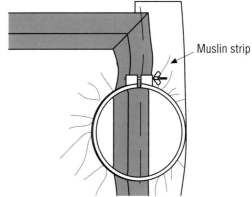

Use a half-hoop equipped with a fabric strip for quilting edges. The ones with adjustable tension screws minimize stretching.

If you are quilting in a frame, consider finishing the two sides attached to the long boards, and then turning the quilt to work the other two sides.

Simple Border Styles
AND APPLICATION TECHNIQUES

Borders fall into three main categories: borders with straight-cut corners, borders with mitered corners, and pieced borders. Within each of these categories are many variations; the most common of the first two types are discussed in detail below.

BORDERS WITH STRAIGHT-CUT CORNERS
Single Border with Straight-Cut Corners

1. Cut strips the desired width of the border, plus seam allowances, along the straight grain.
2. Measure the length of the quilt through the center. Cut two borders that length. (Refer to "Cutting Borders," pages 10–11, for piecing border lengths.)

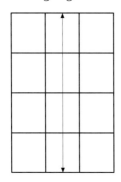

3. Stitch borders to the long edges of the quilt. (Refer to "Adding Borders to the Quilt Top," pages 11–12.) Press seams toward the border. Use a square ruler to make sure the ends are square with the quilt.
4. Measure the new width of the quilt through the center, including the side borders you just added. Cut two borders to that length.
5. Stitch borders to the short edges of the quilt. Square the corners if necessary.

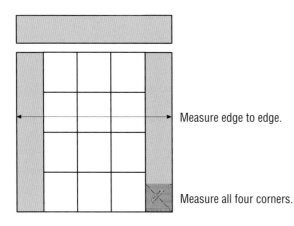

Measure edge to edge.

Measure all four corners.

Multiple Borders with Straight-Cut Corners

Add multiple borders with straight-cut corners one at a time, using the process described for "Single Border with Straight-Cut Corners," above. Add one border and make sure all corners are absolutely square, using your Bias Square ruler or other square ruler. Add the next border in the same way.

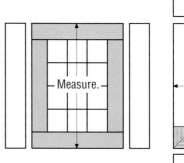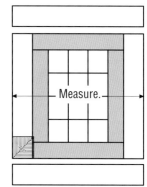

Measure.   Measure.

Borders with Corner Squares

Corner squares may be plain squares of matching or contrasting fabric, or they may be pieced squares of the appropriate size. For design ideas, see "Connect the Corners," pages 21–23.

1. Determine the desired width of the finished borders; add ½" to this measurement for seam allowances.
2. Cut corner squares (or cut and piece, if necessary) to match the measurement determined in step 1.
3. Measure the length of the quilt through the center. Cut two borders to that length, making sure the border ends are perfectly square. Measure the width of the quilt. Cut two borders to that measurement.
4. Sew the borders to the long edges of the quilt. (See "Adding Borders to the Quilt Top," pages 11–12.) Press the seams toward the borders, away from the quilt center.
5. Use a square ruler to make sure the border ends are square with the quilt.
6. Sew corner squares to the ends of each of the short borders. Press the seams away from the squares.
7. Stitch the short borders with corner squares to the

quilt, matching corner-square seams with the long border seams.

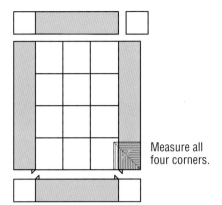

Measure all four corners.

BORDERS WITH MITERED CORNERS
Single Border with Mitered Corners

Before adding a border, be certain each corner of the quilt top is absolutely square. This is the most common problem when mitering corners. Check corners with a Bias Square ruler or drafting triangle.

Make all four corners exactly square.

To be safe, it is a good idea to cut border strips with extra length. To determine the cut length for mitered border strips, add two border widths plus 6".

Example: Cut border strips for a 60" x 70" quilt with a 4"-wide border:

Quilt length	70"
Two border widths	8"
6" for "tails"	6"
Cut length for side borders	84"
Quilt width	**60"**
Two border widths	8"
6" for "tails"	6"
Cut width for top and bottom borders	74"

1. With wrong side up, place a dot at each corner of the quilt, ¼" from each raw edge.
2. Fold the quilt edge in half and mark the center point with a pencil or safety pin.
3. Use your table tape measure to find the distance between the center mark and the corner dot. Write down that number.

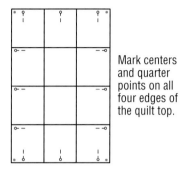

Mark centers and quarter points on all four edges of the quilt top.

4. Fold the border in half and mark the center point with a pencil or safety pin.
5. Measure from the center mark to one end and mark the exact measurement found in step 3. Mark the same distance to the other end.

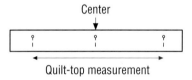

Center

Quilt-top measurement

6. Pin the borders to the quilt edges, matching corresponding center marks and corner dots.
7. Sew a border to one long side of the quilt, beginning and ending exactly at the dots. Lockstitch at the dots. (See "Adding Borders to the Quilt Top," pages 11–12.) Press the seam toward the border. Add the remaining long border in the same manner.

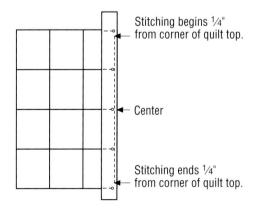

Stitching begins ¼" from corner of quilt top.

Center

Stitching ends ¼" from corner of quilt top.

8. Sew the short borders to the short edges of the quilt, beginning and ending the stitching at the corner dots. The stitching on adjoining border strips should meet but not cross at the corner dot. Adjust if

necessary, and then press the seam toward the border.

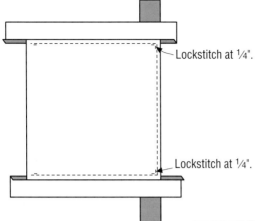

Lockstitch at ¼".

Lockstitch at ¼".

9. Now miter the tails. Working on your ironing surface, lay one corner of the quilt top right side up. Fold the quilt so that the top edge of the border lines up with the side edge and the corner forms a 45° angle. Align the long edges of the tails exactly, right sides together.

10. Keeping the tails aligned, open out the quilt top, folding the top tail at a right angle. Pin to the ironing board to hold in place. Check the angle with a Bias Square ruler or drafting triangle. The outside corner should be exactly 90°, and the diagonal should be exactly 45°. Press the fold firmly. Pin tails together.

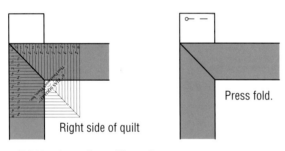

Right side of quilt

Press fold.

Fold border under at 45° angle.

11. Fold the quilt, aligning the top and side borders as before. Stitch exactly along the fold in the border, from inner point to outer edge. Lockstitch at both ends. Check angles and corner again before trimming seam to ¼". Repeat on the other corners.

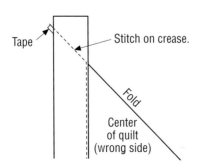

Tape

Stitch on crease.

Fold

Center of quilt (wrong side)

TIP: When the fold is in exactly the right place, tape the fold in place with masking tape. Open the fold, creasing the masking tape, and stitch in the fold line. Remove masking tape immediately.

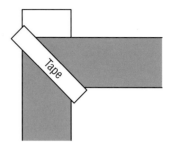

Tape

Multiple Borders with Mitered Corners

Join multiple borders and treat them as one when you add them to the quilt. This saves fabric and time, and requires stitching only one mitered seam at each corner rather than several.

The length of the first border includes the quilt length, plus two border widths, plus 6" for tails. For each new border, add two widths (of the new border) to the cut length of the previous border.

Example: Cut border lengths for a 40" x 40" quilt with a 1", 2", and 3" border:

First Border (1" finished width)

Quilt length	40"
Two border widths	2"
6" for "tails"	6"
Cut length for each border strip	48"

Second Border (2" finished width)

First border length	48"
Two border widths	4"
Cut length for each border strip	52"

Third Border (3" finished width)

Second border length	52"
Two border widths	6"
Cut length for each border strip	58"

1. Cut all the border widths and mark the center of each one. Sew them together in order, matching the centers. Stitch from the center out to each end.

The innermost border will be shorter than the outermost border.

2. Center the border on the quilt edge and pin in the same manner as described for a "Single Border with Mitered Corners," page 15, matching center points and measured end marks.

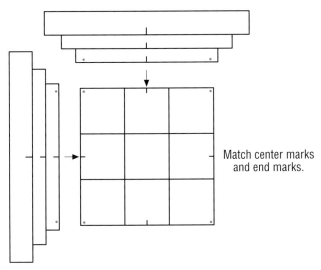

Match center marks and end marks.

3. Miter the corners, taking care to see that each border meets at each corner. For accuracy while stitching, use masking tape to hold them in place. (Refer to Tip on page 16.)

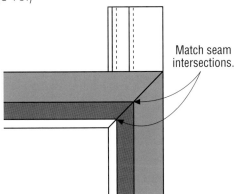

Match seam intersections.

Note: For an interesting variation, try two mitered borders with alternate values.

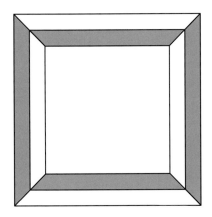

LOG CABIN BORDERS

There are three reasons to use this border style: to save fabric, to continue the design in a Log Cabin quilt, or to change value for a shaded effect. This border requires the use of a partial seam during application.

1. Measure the length of the quilt through the center, including seam allowances. Add the finished width of one border to the quilt-length measurement. Cut two borders equaling that length (borders #2 and #4 in the illustration).

2. Measure the width of the quilt through the center. Add the width of one border to the quilt-width measurement. Cut two borders equaling that length (borders #1 and #3 in the illustration).

3. With right sides together, pin border strip #1 to the top edge of the quilt. Begin stitching, 2" from the edge of the quilt. Press the seam toward the border. Sew remaining borders to the quilt in numerical order.

4. Complete the unstitched section of the first border seam.

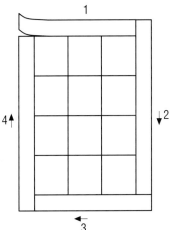

STRIPED-FABRIC BORDERS

Stripes make interesting borders, but they require special treatment. There are three common variations.

Borders Cut Across the Stripe with Mitered Corners

Miter the corners, matching the stripes. If there is a dominant stripe, make sure to match it in the miter by starting the mitered seam on that stripe.

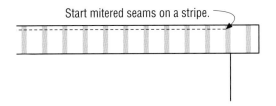

Start mitered seams on a stripe.

To start the seam on a dominant stripe, you may need to adjust the border strip. Adjust the length along the side, making a seam in a less dominant stripe. For example, in a fabric with dark stripes on a light background, make a seam in the light background where it will be less obvious.

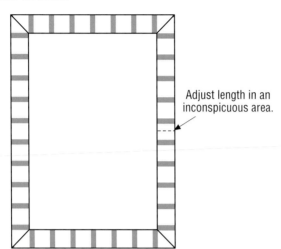

Adjust length in an inconspicuous area.

If necessary, make several narrow seams in the strip at various locations so that the adjustment is as inconspicuous as possible. To piece planned border lengths, use a straight seam rather than a diagonal one. It will be less conspicuous, and you will not have to worry about matching stripes.

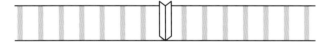

Piece border lengths with a straight seam.

Borders Cut Along the Stripe

Cut only one border strip at a time, using the stripe as a cutting guide. Place the ¼" line of your ruler on the stripe that you want to use, and then cut the seam allowance outside of the stripe.

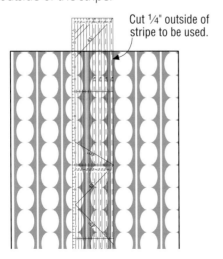

Cut ¼" outside of stripe to be used.

Fold the stripe in various places to find a pleasing area to miter. To match mitering points, adjust the border length in an inconspicuous part of the stripe.

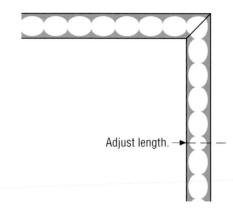

Adjust length. →

TIP: If the adjustment is minimal, you can use a spacing border to adjust the size of the quilt so that the striped border fits without piecing. (See "Spacing Borders," pages 23–24.)

Unbroken Stripes Across the Quilt

Cut two borders across the stripe and two borders along the length of the stripe. The border will appear as a complete unit, interrupted by the quilt center. Sew to the quilt top as described for "Single Border with Straight-Cut Corners," page 14.

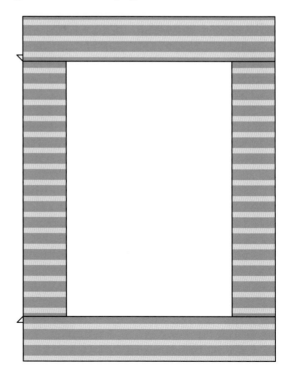

MULTI-FABRIC BORDERS

Here's one last thought about simple borders. Who says you must use only one piece of fabric for a simple border? You can break up the length of the border with many fabrics that look similar. For a black border, use many black prints. For a red border, use many red prints. Cut random lengths and sew them together end to end, and then cut the needed border lengths. From a distance, the quilt appears to have a plain, straight border. Closer inspection reveals an interesting variation, and you use more of your fabric collection.

TIP: Put longer pieces on the ends of each pieced border to allow for cutting exact lengths. You don't want to end up with a tiny piece of one fabric at the corner.

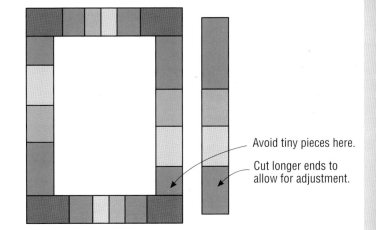

Avoid tiny pieces here.

Cut longer ends to allow for adjustment.

Pieced Border Planning

PLANNING BASICS

Pieced borders add wonderful complexity to any quilt without too much difficulty on your part. The secret to planning a pieced border to fit your quilt top is dividing the side measurement of the quilt into units. Once the unit size is determined, it can be divided and combined into unlimited designs.

There are three basic steps required to plan a successful pieced border: Divide the Side, Use the Unit, and Connect the Corners. These are discussed in detail below, along with two other planning considerations, Even-Odd Distribution and Spacing Borders.

Divide the Side

Measure the quilt through the center and subtract ½" for seam allowances. If the quilt is square, the length and width measurements are the same. For your border-unit length, choose a number that divides evenly into the quilt-top measurement. Most quilts have side measurements that divide into common units. Find a size that is easily used for cutting; i.e., a whole number or a whole number and a fraction no smaller than ¼". If you just can't find a common unit size, consider using a spacing border. (See "Spacing Borders," pages 23–24.)

If your quilt is rectangular, you will have two different measurements, one for length and one for width. It's easier if both measurements have a common divisor. Suppose the length is 70" and the width is 60". Both can be divided by 5. Easy! You need fourteen 5" units along the sides and twelve 5" units along the top and bottom. Both of those measurements also divide by 2. You would need thirty-five 2" units (70" ÷ 2) on each long side, and thirty 2" units (60" ÷ 2) on each short side.

Divide the sides
into equal units.

Use the Unit

After determining the unit measurement, draw the border on graph paper and decide how wide the unit will be.

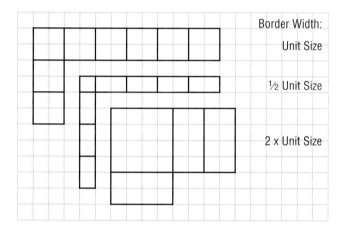

Divide the unit into interesting shapes. Each of the units can have several divisions.

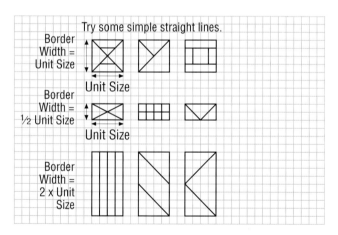

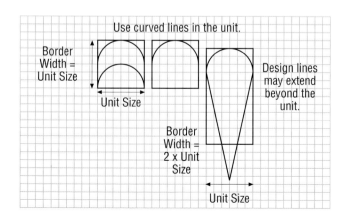

TIP: For curved lines, cut several pieces of paper the size of the unit. Fold in half and cut a curve. When you have a pleasing curve, use it as a full-size pattern.

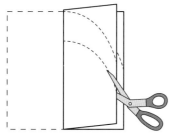

When you have a unit design, try it out in rows. Draw several on graph paper or use a photocopy machine to make several copies of your unit. Cut out your copies and paste them in rows on graph paper. Use a pencil and play with light and dark values.

TIP: Try using a computer drawing program to design pieced borders. It's a great way to help you envision the interaction of these units!

Try the following variations with your unit design.

Repeat a single unit.

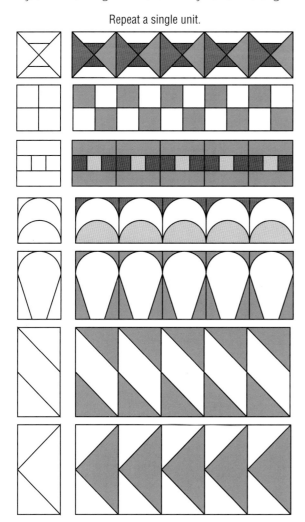

Reverse every other unit (even number of units).

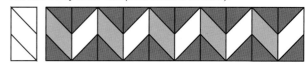

Reverse half of the units (even number of units).

Alternate two different units (odd number of units).

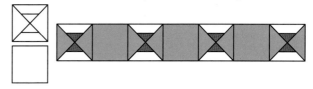

Use two rows of the same unit.

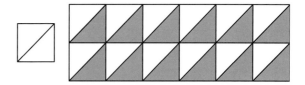

Use pairs of the same unit to create a design.

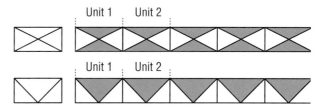

Connect the Corners

After you are satisfied with the pieced border design you have created, consider the corners. The corner is a square, the same width as the borders.

Unity is the key to designing good corners. The corner design should relate to the side borders so that the entire border design flows around the corners without interruption.

Some pieced borders are complete with a simple square of the background fabric.

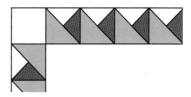

Four Patch and Ninepatch blocks are other options for simple corner treatments.

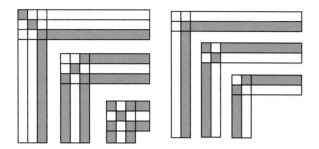

For a more complicated pieced border, find some element of the side-border design to extend into the corner. Continue the design around it. Work on graph paper and draw your border design to scale.

1. On your design drawing, draw in a corner square.
2. Find a spot on the edge of the square that will touch a border design element.
3. Work from that spot to "connect" the two sides.

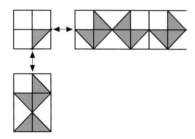

If the corner design seems too small, borrow a unit from each side to create a more pleasing effect. Sometimes a half-unit can be taken from each side, which gives the corner design more space and reduces the number of units on each side by one. Flowing appliqué designs often require this sort of adjustment.

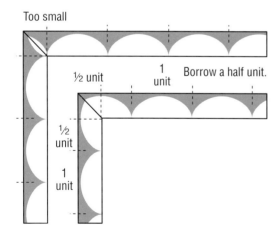

Too small

½ unit

1 unit

Borrow a half unit.

½ unit

1 unit

With multiple borders that have straight-cut corners, you can connect each border side by matching the corner and border fabrics.

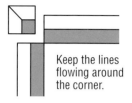

Keep the lines flowing around the corner.

To integrate your overall design:

❖ Use a block from the quilt for the border corner.

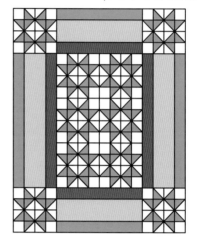

❖ Change the background color to match the borders coming into the corners. The block blends into the borders and connects to the quilt. (See "Ribbon Star, straight borders with quilt block corners," page 34.)

Here are some additional examples of corner treatments for borders with straight-cut corners.

❖ Use a corner element that seems to explode outward to create a border design that radiates from the center of the quilt.

Corners can explode outward.

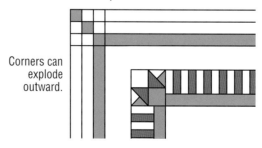

❖ Use a corner element that closes off the border design to contain or enclose the quilt.

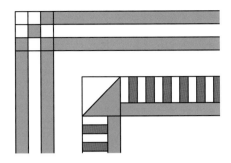

❖ Sew a strip of fabric to adjacent sides of a square and miter the corner. The width of the strips depends on the border design that the corner must match. See "Borders with Mitered Corners," page 15, for mitering techniques. Position the square so that it becomes an integral part of the border.

Add mitered strips.

Position mitered corner to integrate with the border design.

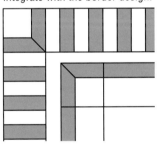

Even-Odd Distribution

Even and odd numbers of units create different design possibilities. If a border contains an even number of units, you can match pairs or create mirror-images of single units or rows of units. With an odd number of units, the same block appears at each end of the border. If you want to alternate dark and light squares, you can have a dark square at both ends. Or, you can grade values from the center out to each side.

Suppose you need an even (or odd) number of units on each side and the measurement of the quilt sides divides into an even number of units, but the top and bottom measurement divides into an odd number of units.

Here are three ways to handle it:

❖ Make the units on the long sides slightly different from those on the short sides. This works well with appliqué repeats, where slight variations are unnotice-

able. You can accomplish this with paper folding. (See "Appliqué Borders," page 48.)

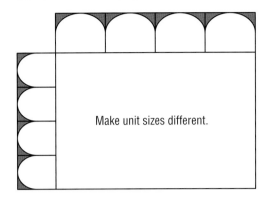

Make unit sizes different.

❖ Add a spacing border to the quilt. (See "Spacing Borders," pages 23–24.)

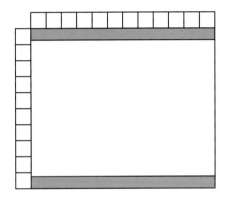

❖ Adjust at the center point. (See "Sawtooth Borders," page 26.)

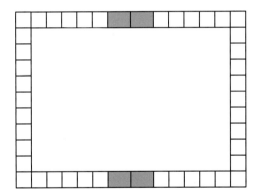

Spacing Borders

Sometimes it is necessary to use spacing borders to overcome border design challenges. Solutions for two common problems follow.

Problem #1: The units that fit along the length or width of the quilt will not fit along the other dimension.

Solution: If the border is too long, add a spacing border that makes the quilt side longer. If the border is too short, add one border unit and add a spacing border to make the quilt side the right length.

For example, one quilt side divides evenly by 3. The other side has 2" left over. Divide the leftover 2" by 2 and make spacing borders 1" wide. *Don't forget to add ½" for seam allowances when you cut the spacing border strips.*

If the leftover amount is less than 2", add one more unit to make the spacing border more manageable. For example, one quilt side divides evenly by 3. The other side has 1" left over, requiring a tiny (½" wide) spacing border on each side. If you add one more 3" unit to the border you will have an extra 4". Spacing borders 2" wide are easier to apply. Cut border strips 2 ½" wide to include seam allowances.

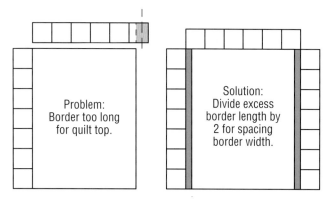

Problem: Border too long for quilt top.

Solution: Divide excess border length by 2 for spacing border width.

That problem is solved, but now the quilt looks strange with a spacing border on only two sides. Add one unit to the other two borders. Then add a spacing border to the other two sides, wide enough to compensate for the extra unit. When adding spacing borders, you need to remember a simple formula: Leftover inches ÷ 2 = Finished Spacing Border Width. Be sure to add ½" for seam allowances when you cut the border strips.

The slight variation in width of the spacing borders is less noticeable if they are the same fabric as the background of the quilt or the same fabric as the border pieces they touch.

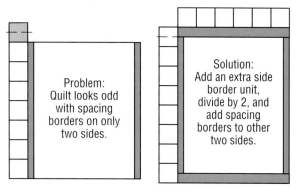

Problem: Quilt looks odd with spacing borders on only two sides.

Solution: Add an extra side border unit, divide by 2, and add spacing borders to other two sides.

Problem #2: The units fit both quilt dimensions evenly, but one side has an even number of units, and the other side has an odd number of units. The design you've chosen needs the same configuration on each side.

Solution: Add a spacing border to allow one more unit on whichever side is necessary. Using the quilt-center background fabric makes this less noticeable.

Calculating Spacing Borders

1. Measure the quilt.

2. Divide the side to find the unit size.

3. Find the number of units.

_____ ÷ _____ = _____
Quilt side   Unit size   Number of units

4. Find the leftover inches.

_____ x _____ = _____
Unit size   Number of units   Border size

_____ − _____ = _____
Quilt side   Border size   Leftover inches

5. Find the width of the spacing borders.

_____ ÷ 2 = _____
Leftover inches   Width of spacing borders

Note: If this spacing border is very narrow (½" or less), add one unit to the border and refigure.

Pieced Border POSSIBILITIES

Here are some ideas for frequently used pieced borders. Use these for your quilts, or use them as inspiration for designing your own special pieced borders. General piecing directions are included for each border.

CHECKERBOARD BORDERS

This border design requires many small units, with an uneven number of units on each side.

1. Divide the side of the quilt to find the unit size. (See page 20.)
2. Cut one fabric strip equaling the border-unit width plus ½" for seam allowances.
3. Cut a strip of a contrasting fabric the same width.
4. Sew the strips together lengthwise. Press the seam toward the darker fabric.
5. Crosscut segments from the strip-pieced unit the width of the border unit plus ½" for seam allowances.

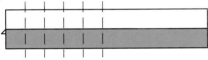

Cross-cut segments = cut strip width

TIP: Use the seam line, not the cut edge, as a guide for crosscutting exact right angles.

6. Sew these segments together in pairs, alternating dark and light squares. Add one single segment to one end, so that the end of each border is the same.

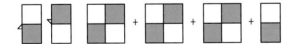

Add a single segment at the end of each border strip.

7. Join two segments for each corner to make checkerboard corners.

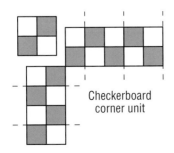

Checkerboard corner unit

SAWTOOTH BORDERS

One of the most-loved traditional pieced borders is the sawtooth border. The unit for this border begins with a square that is then divided into triangles.

1. Divide the side of the quilt to find the unit size. (See page 20.) Each unit must be a square.
2. Divide each unit into half-square triangles.
3. Make rows of half-square triangle units for the border.

There are several ways to use Sawtooth borders to create interesting designs. Try a single Sawtooth border, a double one, or several, divided by plain borders. Try a larger Sawtooth border and a smaller one.

Single Sawtooth Border

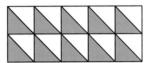

Double Sawtooth Border

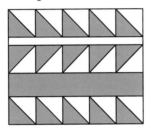

Sawtooth Borders Separated by Plain Border Strips

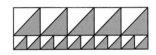

Large and Small Sawtooth Borders Combined

In many old-fashioned quilts with Sawtooth borders, the half-square rectangles just keep going around the quilt, letting the corners fall where they may.

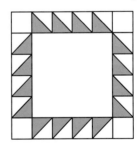

Old-Fashioned Haphazard Corners

For consistent corners, reverse the direction of the points at the border's center.

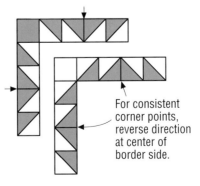

For consistent corner points, reverse direction at center of border side.

25

On quilt sides with an even number of units, half the units point in one direction and half point in the other direction. If the quilt sides have an odd number of units and half of the units turn to the right and half turn to the left, one unit is left over.

This is the time to consider the all-important center point, to create a center unit that blends the two halves, or is an entirely different element. Try a solid square. Use a fabric that continues the border without interruption.

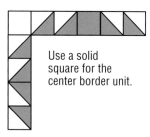

Use a solid square for the center border unit.

If the border unit is large enough, the center unit can be divided into a "star point," or any other design that blends the two directions.

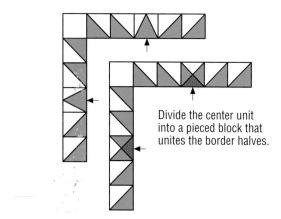

Divide the center unit into a pieced block that unites the border halves.

With this in mind, you can treat the three center units as one, allowing more space to make the transition. You may also use a center-point transition on only two sides of the quilt, dividing the entire border into two halves for an interesting effect.

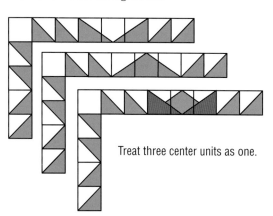

Treat three center units as one.

Making Bias-Square Units

There are several different ways to make half-square rectangles. Here is one of the simplest methods.

1. Cut the squares of fabric, of contrasting colors, the size of your border unit plus $\frac{7}{8}$".
2. Cut squares diagonally to form triangles.
3. Join contrasting triangles to form half-square triangle units. Press the seam toward the darker triangle.

TIP: Layer squares of contrasting fabrics right sides together before cutting, so that the triangles will already be in pairs and in position for sewing.

For example, if your unit size is 3", cut contrasting squares $3\frac{7}{8}$" x $3\frac{7}{8}$". Cut them diagonally and sew the contrasting triangles together, resulting in half-square units that measure $3\frac{1}{2}$" x $3\frac{1}{2}$", which is your unit size plus $\frac{1}{2}$" for seam allowances.

For more information on quick piecing half-square triangles, refer to *Quick and Easy Quiltmaking*, co-published by That Patchwork Place and Rodale Press.

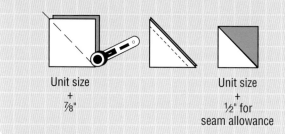

Unit size + $\frac{7}{8}$"

Unit size + $\frac{1}{2}$" for seam allowance

SHARP-ANGLED SAWTOOTH BORDERS

Sometimes called "Dogtooth," this is a dramatic border for any quilt. It requires half-rectangle units.

1. Divide the side of the quilt to find the unit size. (See page 20.) You need an even number of units.
2. Plan a border that is wider than the unit size so that each unit is a rectangle.
3. Draw a line in the rectangle from corner to corner.
4. Change the direction of the triangles at the centers of the borders, so that each side has two halves that are mirror images of each other.
5. Piece the required number of units. Note that when you reverse asymmetrical units, you must piece the units with angles reversed. (See "Making Half-Rectangle Units," page 27.)

6. Adjust the center point if necessary. (See "Sawtooth Borders," page 26.)
7. Connect the corners with a plain square or a smaller square surrounded by mitered strips. (See "Connect the Corners," pages 21–23.)

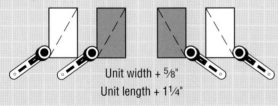

Use a plain corner square.

Use a small corner square with mitered strips.

Reverse triangles at center for mirror-image border halves.

Border Unit

Making Half-Rectangle Units

1. Determine the finished measurements of the rectangular border unit. Add 5⁄8" to the short side and 1 1⁄4" to the long side. From contrasting fabrics, cut pairs of rectangles this size.
2. Cut rectangles diagonally. *To make reversed or mirror-image half-rectangle units, cut pairs of rectangles apart on the opposite diagonal.*

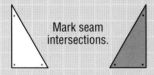

Unit width + 5⁄8"
Unit length + 1 1⁄4"

3. Using a sharp pencil, mark the seam intersections on the wrong side of each rectangle.

Mark seam intersections.

4. Pin contrasting rectangles together, carefully matching seam intersections. Stitch; press seam toward darker rectangle.

Finished rectangle = Unit size + 1⁄2" for seam allowances

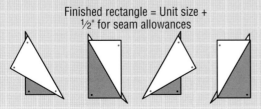

The pieced rectangles will measure the same as the finished border units plus 1⁄2" for seam allowances. For example, if the border unit measures 2 1⁄2" x 4", cut the contrasting rectangles 3 1⁄8" x 5 1⁄4". Cut them apart diagonally and join contrasting triangles to make rectangles measuring 3" x 4 1⁄2".

For more information on quick-piecing these rectangular units, see *Angle Antics* by Mary Hickey or *Shortcuts* by Donna Lynn Thomas, both published by That Patchwork Place.

FLYING GEESE BORDERS

The traditional Flying Geese pattern is even more versatile as a border than it is in the center of a quilt.

1. Divide the side of the quilt to find the unit size (See page 20.)
2. Double the unit width to create a rectangular unit.
3. Draw the unit on graph paper and mark the halfway point along one long side of the unit.
4. Connect the mark with the opposite corners.

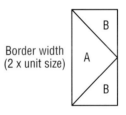

Border width
(2 x unit size)

A

B

B

Unit size

There are a number of ways to use flying-geese units in borders. Make rows of geese units for each border strip. Try all the geese going the same direction or divide the geese units at the border centers.

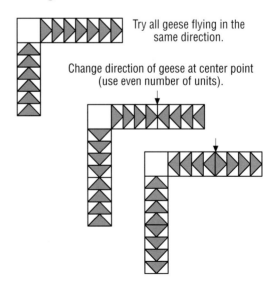

Try all geese flying in the same direction.

Change direction of geese at center point (use even number of units).

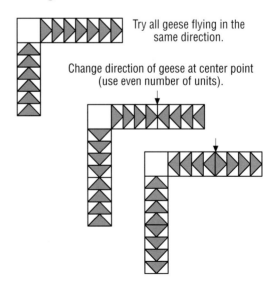

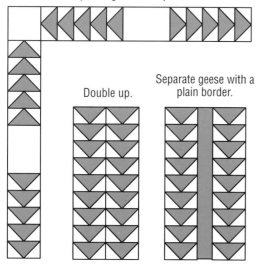

Separate geese with plain fabric.

Double up.

Separate geese with a plain border.

TIP: Break up rows of geese with plain pieces of fabric to adjust the border length and avoid using a spacing border.

Making Flying Geese Blocks

1. For large triangles (A), cut a square of fabric that measures 2 x Unit Size + 1¼". Cut the square twice diagonally to yield 4 large triangles. Use one of these large triangles for each border unit.

2. For small triangles (B), cut a square that measures Unit Size + ⅞". Cut the square once diagonally to yield two small triangles. Use two for each border unit.

3. Assemble as shown and sew units together into rows.

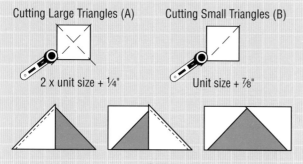

Cutting Large Triangles (A)

2 x unit size + ¼"

Cutting Small Triangles (B)

Unit size + ⅞"

For example, if your unit size is 3", the border width will be 6". Cut squares 7¼" x 7¼", and then cut them twice diagonally for the large triangles. Cut squares 3⅞" x 3⅞", and then cut them once diagonally for the small triangles. The Flying Geese block will measure 3½" x 6½" when assembled (unit size + ½" for seam allowances).

Multistrip
BORDERS

Piecing these great-looking borders is easy. With a little planning, you can rotary cut and quick piece them in a flash.

1. Divide the side of the quilt to find the unit size. (See page 20.)
2. Cut strips of fabric from the quilt leftovers, cutting them the width of the unit size plus ½" for seam allowances. For example, a quilt that divides into 2" units along the side would have a multistrip border of 2"-wide finished strips (cut 2½").
3. Determine the border width. Cut fabric strips that length plus ½" for seam allowances. (To add a 3"-wide border, cut the strips 3½" long.)
4. Sew the strips together in pairs and join pairs to create border strips of the correct length.
5. Press all seams in one direction, pressing on the right side of the border. Line up one edge of the border with the grid or line on your ironing board cover to avoid distorting it to a curve. (See "Pressing Borders," pages 12–13.)

For a scrappy look, sew the strips together with random fabric placement, just picking up strips without too much thought. This works well in a quilt with blocks that have a multi-fabric background, or with fabrics of similar value. (See "Ribbon Star with multistrip border," page 33.)

For a planned look, sew long strips together, cross-cut them to the border width (plus seam allowances), and sew those together so that the fabrics repeat in the same sequence around the quilt.

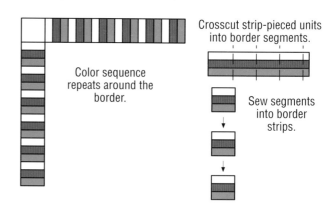

Color sequence repeats around the border.

Crosscut strip-pieced units into border segments.

Sew segments into border strips.

Gallery

Edgewise by Paulette Peters, 1993, Elkhorn, Nebraska, 36" x 36". Paulette added the following borders to the central pieced block: a spacing border, a sawtooth border, a spacing border, an "on-point" border, an appliquéd swag border, and an exterior appliquéd sawtooth border.

Garden Squares by Patty Kennedy, 1993, Omaha, Nebraska, 80" x 110". Patty transformed her swag border with a wonderful background. She turned four-patch units "on point" and added a multistrip border. (See "Appliqué Over Piecing," page 53.) Patty used invisible machine appliqué, which she teaches at her quilt shop, The Log Cabin, in Omaha. The appliqué patterns were adapted from the *Garden Window* pattern pack by Carolann M. Palmer, published by That Patchwork Place.

Friendly Stars by Paulette Peters and friends, 1990, Elkhorn, Nebraska, 30" x 42". The stars are friendship blocks sent to Paulette by many friends. She divided the setting squares into half-square triangles to form the border. It's a border that isn't a border. (See "Pieced Blocks on Point," page 41.)

White Tulips by Paulette Peters, 1993, Elkhorn, Nebraska, 48" x 48". Paulette added the following borders to the central Tulip block: an interior appliquéd sawtooth edge, a straight border with corner blocks, a narrow mitered border, a folded insert, and a two-unit scalloped border.

Bordering Insanity by Cheryl Sebelius Nelson, 1989, Fremont, Nebraska, 24" x 24". Borders don't have to be on the edge. Cheryl's borders took over her entire quilt.

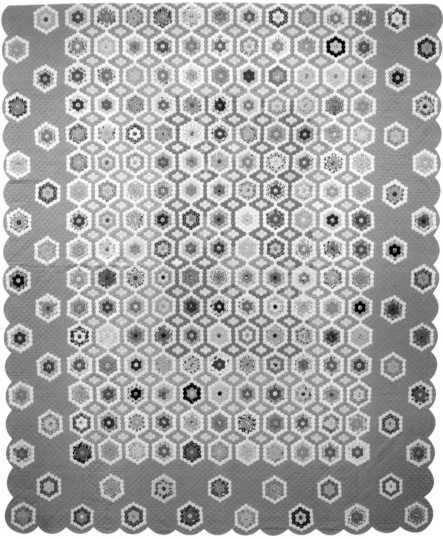

Grandmother's Flower Garden by Martha Peters, 1988, Gordon, Nebraska, 84" x 102". Martha purchased these tiny hexagons at an auction and pieced them by hand. She appliquéd the edge to a straight border and then scalloped the straight border. The plain border balances the active center, and the "flowers" sprinkled across the border unify the design. (See "Quilts with Uneven Edges," page 53.) Collection of Terry Peters.

Through the Trellis Garden Again
by Joanne Traise, 1994, Omaha, Nebraska, 45" x 45". Joanne designed an award-winning raffle quilt for Cottonwood Quilters and made this smaller version for herself. She integrated the appliquéd border with the pieced center by placing the vine and flowers in the white spaces along the block edges.

Antique Irish Chain with Diamond Borders, origin unknown, purchased in Utah, 78" x 78". This beautiful border lifts an ordinary quilt into a spectacular display. (See "Diamond Borders," page 44.) Collection of Terry and Paulette Peters.

Ribbon Star Series by Paulette Peters, 1993, Elkhorn, Nebraska.
Stepped border, 25" x 33".

Ribbon Star Series by Paulette Peters, 1993, Elkhorn, Nebraska. **Quilt block border**, 26" x 34".

Ribbon Star Series by Paulette Peters, 1993, Elkhorn, Nebraska. **Multistrip border**, 22" x 30".

Ribbon Star Series by Paulette Peters, 1993, Elkhorn, Nebraska. **Asymmetrical borders** with extending design elements, 19" x 27".

Ribbon Star Series by Paulette Peters, 1993, Elkhorn, Nebraska. **Straight borders with quilt block corners**, 32" x 40".

Ribbon Star Series by Paulette Peters, 1993, Elkhorn, Nebraska. **Overlapping points border** with three-dimensional effect, 20" x 28".

Ribbon Star Series by Paulette Peters, 1993, Elkhorn, Nebraska. **Half-block border**, 27" x 35".

Consider using just two fabrics for a striped look. Use an uneven number of units, starting and ending with the same color on each side.

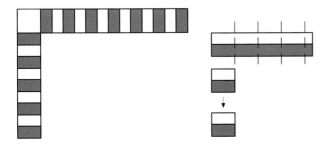

Consider grading the value from dark to light or light to dark on each side.

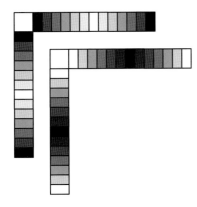

Half-square triangle units or squares with mitered corner strips make nice corners for multistrip borders. (See "Connect the Corners," page 21, and "Making Bias-Square Units," page 26.)

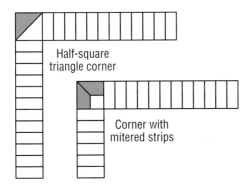

Half-square triangle corner

Corner with mitered strips

TIP: If the strips will be the outside edge of the quilt border, run a line of machine basting in the ¼"-wide seam allowance to keep the edges from stretching or coming unstitched during quilting. The binding will cover the basting.

MULTISTRIP/TRIANGLE BORDERS

Add a triangle to one end of each strip in a multistrip border for a dimensional effect.

1. Divide the side of the quilt to find the unit size. (See page 20.) You need an even number of units for each side. Add ½" to the unit measurement for seam allowances.
2. Determine the border width. Add ½" to this measurement for seam allowances.
3. Cut fabric strips (42" x the unit size + seam allowances) and crosscut into pieces the measurement of the border width plus seam allowances. For example, if the unit size is 2" and the border width is 3½", cut strips 2½" x 42". Crosscut into 2½" x 4" pieces.
4. From contrasting fabric, cut one square for each fabric strip, the same width as the strip. (For example, if the strip is 2½" x 4", cut squares 2½" x 2½".)
5. Fold the squares diagonally and press.
6. With right sides together, stitch a square to one end of each rectangle, using the fold line as the seam line. Alternate the seam direction for every other rectangle. Trim away the excess fabric ¼" from the seam line.

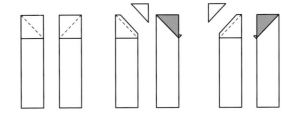

7. Sew together in pairs as shown. Then sew pairs together to form borders.

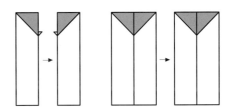

8. Place triangles next to the quilt center or at the outside edge of the quilt. Add corner squares. Some ideas are shown in the illustrations below.

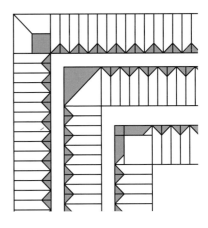

MOCK BEADED BORDERS

In this easy-to-piece border, light fabric squares, surrounded by dark squares and strips, glow like beads along the edges of the quilt.

1. Divide the side of the quilt to find the unit size. (See page 20.) Use an odd number of units so that each side begins and ends with the same fabric.
2. Use two fabrics, one dark, one light. Cut long strips from each fabric, the width of the unit measurement plus seam allowances. (For example, assume that you are using 1" units. Add seam allowances and cut the strips 1½" wide.)
3. Sew the strips together lengthwise and press seams toward the dark fabric.
4. Crosscut the strip-pieced unit into segments that are the same width as the original cut strips (1½" in the example).

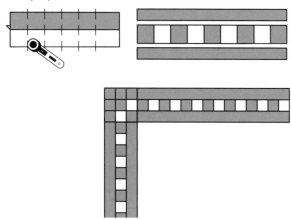

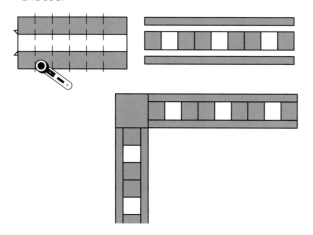

5. Sew these units together, alternating dark and light, to create border strips of the required lengths. Make sure each border begins and ends with a dark square.
6. Sew a strip of dark fabric to each side of your beaded border. These strips can be any width you choose.

STEPPED BORDERS

Try making a multistrip border into stairsteps of contrasting fabrics, using asymmetrical units that repeat around the quilt. The width of the border depends on the number of sections in each unit and the size of the "step."

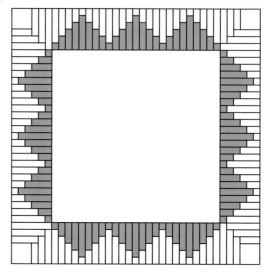

1. Divide the side of the quilt into large units. If the side does not divide evenly, use the leftover inches in step 4, page 37.
2. Draw the border unit on graph paper. Divide the unit into an even number of sections. Six, eight, or ten sections work well. Number the sections.

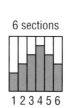

6 sections

1 2 3 4 5 6

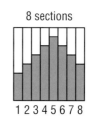

8 sections

1 2 3 4 5 6 7 8

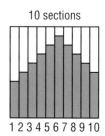

10 sections

1 2 3 4 5 6 7 8 9 10

3. Divide each section horizontally into stairsteps, starting with the shortest step on the left. Each step up or down is an equal increment (¾" or 1" is a good measurement to use).

Note that in each unit the highest stairstep is one strip to the right of the center line (strip #4, in a 6-strip unit, for example). When you join the stairstep units, the first section on the left side of the adjoining unit will complete the pattern.

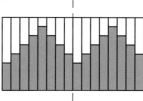

4. Join stairstep units to make border strips of the appropriate length. On the right end of each border, add one final strip that matches the far left section (step) in the units. Were there leftover inches when you divided the sides of the quilt to find the unit size? Use them to add this extra section. If not, add a spacing border to supply extra inches for the final stairstep strip. (See "Spacing Borders," pages 23–24.)

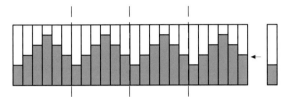

For example, a 64" quilt side divides into six 10" units, with 4" left over. Each 10" unit divides into 8 sections (steps) that are 1¼" wide. Make one more 1¼"-wide section for the end and subtract it from the 4". Now the amount left over is 2¾". Add a spacing border to adjust the quilt top. (See "Spacing Borders," pages 23–24.)

If, after subtracting the end section, the amount left over is 1" or less, add it to the center point of the border. If there is an uneven number of units, the center point will be the tallest step. If there is an even number of units, the center point will be the shortest step.

Widen the tallest step for an uneven number of units.

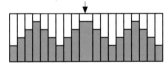

Widen the shortest step for an even number of units.

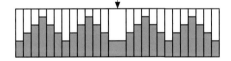

For example, the quilt side measures 62" long. The amount left over is 2" and you need 1¼" for the extra step. That leaves ¾". Make the step at the center point of the border 2" wide (1¼" + ¾"). Don't forget to add seam allowances when cutting.

Piecing a Stepped Border

Make a "set-up panel" for each section or step to quick-cut stepped borders.
1. Determine the measurement of the two pieces of the step and add ½" for seam allowances.
2. From each of two contrasting fabrics, cut

one or more 42"-long strips that measure the width of the step pieces. The number of strips will depend upon the number of sections required for the border.
3. Sew the strips together as shown.
4. Crosscut into segments the width of the step section plus ½" for seam allowances. Repeat this process for each step section of the unit. Remember that there will be two of some of the step sections in each unit.

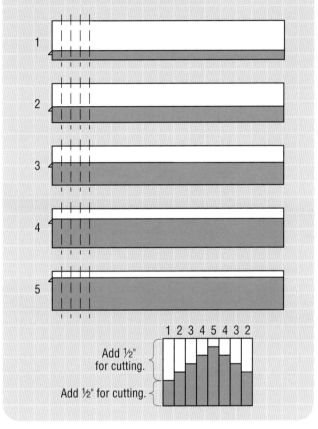

Add ½" for cutting.

Add ½" for cutting.

If the border fabric is busy, cut corners as simple squares. Or, piece strips of fabric into a square to unify the corner and border sides. A Half–Log Cabin block is a good corner for this border.

Making Half–Log Cabin Corner Blocks

1. From a single fabric, cut strips the same width as the step-section width plus ½" for seam allowances. From one of these strips, crosscut four squares, one for each corner of the quilt.
2. Place the squares on top of a fabric strip,

right sides together. Position them as close together as possible without overlapping edges. Stitch. Cut between squares, trimming away any excess fabric between the units. Press the seams away from the center square.

3. Sew another strip to the side of the squares. Cut and trim; press seams away from the squares.

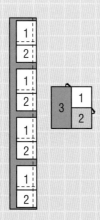

4. Sew a strip next to the first strip, cut and trim; press seams away from the square.

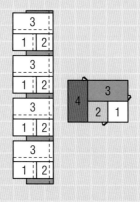

5. Add strips to adjacent sides of the growing square in numerical order until the corner square is the same size as the border width.

Multiple
QUILT BLOCK BORDERS

Quilt blocks make excellent pieced-border units. Use them "on the edge" in creative ways. Repeat the blocks in the quilt or use related blocks.

❖ Make half-sized blocks if the blocks in the quilt are fairly large and simple. The border blocks will fit two to each center block if there is no sashing in the quilt. (See "Ribbon Star, with quilt block border," page 33.)

Use half-size blocks.

❖ Change the background fabric in the blocks around the quilt edge to stop the eye and create the illusion of an added border that really isn't there.

❖ In the outside blocks, use lighter or darker values of the colors used in the center blocks. This interrupts the pattern across the surface and serves as a border.

Fool the eye with a color change in the outer blocks.

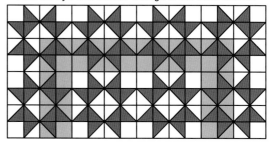

❖ Use blocks with long points to give the illusion of curves.

❖ Change colors in every other block.

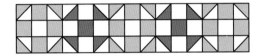

❖ Let the blocks create their own design as they interact.

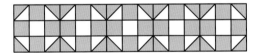

❖ Do you want to separate the border blocks? If so, borrow one border unit to account for separating strips. For example, if your unit size is 6" and there are 5 units on each side, four of the units will be quilt blocks. Divide the remaining required unit by 3 to find the required finished width for the separating strips. Add ½" for seam allowances and cut strips that width.

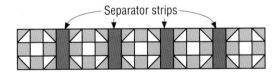

Separator strips

TIP: If you want to use a particular size for the border block and it doesn't divide evenly into the quilt measurement, use a spacing border to make the quilt the required size. (See "Spacing Borders," pages 23–24.) Remember, border blocks that are larger than the center blocks are not as success- ful as ones that are smaller. They overwhelm the center rather than enhance it.

LOG CABIN BORDERS

Log Cabin blocks are great for borders. Make them half light, half dark, with contrasting center squares. You need an even number of units on each quilt side to use Log Cabin blocks as a border.

1. Divide the side of the quilt to find the unit size. (See page 20.) This will be the finished size of your Log Cabin block.
2. Log Cabin blocks require an even number of logs, counting from one side of the block to the other. Divide the unit by the desired number of logs *plus 1* (for the center square). If you cannot divide the unit evenly by the number of logs plus the center square, add the remainder to the center of the Log Cabin block. For example, divide an 8" block by 7 (6 logs plus the center square). Each of the logs will be 1" wide, and the center will be 2" wide (1" plus the remainder of 1").

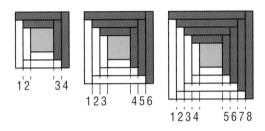

3. Make the blocks, referring to "Constructing Log Cabin Blocks," page 40.
4. Make four Log Cabin blocks for the corners, then arrange the border, using one of the following variations.

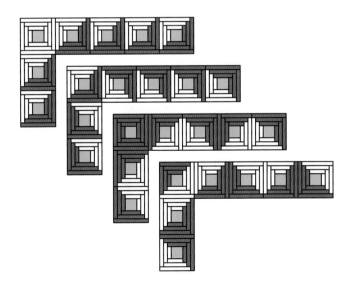

Constructing Log Cabin Blocks

1. Cut center-square fabric strips the width of the finished center square plus ½" for seam allowances. The number of strips you need depends upon the number of blocks you plan to make. For a block with a 2" finished center square and 1" finished logs, cut 2½"-wide strips for the center square.

2. Cut strips of light and dark fabrics the finished width of the logs plus ½" for seam allowances (1½" in the example). The number of strips to cut depends upon the required number of blocks.

3. Join the center-square strip and the first log strip lengthwise. Press seams away from the center-square strip and crosscut segments the width of the center square strip (2½" in the example).

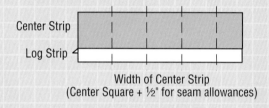

Center Strip

Log Strip

Width of Center Strip
(Center Square + ½" for seam allowances)

4. Add a second log strip of the same value as the first (light or dark). Place the units you created in step 3 on the second log strip, right sides together, and stitch as shown. Make sure to place the unit so that the first log is closest to you. Press toward the newest log strip and cut apart units using a ruler and a rotary cutter.

5. Continue adding logs, alternating two light strips and two dark strips, until you have the desired number of logs. Always place the most recently added log closest to you, and always press seam allowances toward the newest log.

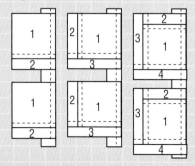

INTERIOR BORDERS

If you want to set off a row of blocks around the outside of the quilt, add an interior border.

1. Construct the number of blocks you need to fit each side of the quilt. Sew them together into border strips.

2. Cut strips the width of the desired interior border plus ½" for seam allowances. Sew a strip to the inner edge of each pieced border.

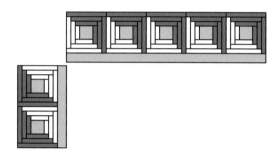

Now adjust the corners. Add spacing strips to two sides of each corner, the same width as the interior border. You can achieve different effects depending on the colors you use.

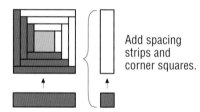

Add spacing strips and corner squares.

For a free-floating effect, use fabrics from the quilt block for the spacing strips on the corner squares. Cut the spacing strips the width of the interior border plus ½" for seam allowances. Sew a strip to the inner edge of the corner block. Cut a square from the interior border fabric the width of the interior border plus ½" for seam allowances. Add it to the other spacing strip before sewing it to the other inner edge of the corner block. Notice how the colors of the spacing strips differ depending on the orientation of the corner Log Cabin blocks.

To create a windowpane effect, use the interior-border fabric for all the spacing strips. This design is particularly effective in scrap quilts and Log Cabin quilts, where many fabrics appear to melt together. Add a strip the same width as the interior border to each of the two inner sides of the corner blocks, so that the interior border appears to extend to the edge of the quilt. In Log Cabin quilts, make the interior border the same width as the logs and simply add one more round of logs to two sides of the corner blocks. They will appear to float outside the interior border.

PIECED BLOCKS ON POINT

Sometimes you can turn an element or block in the quilt on point and use it in the border. Four Patch blocks, Ninepatch blocks, or half-square triangle units, turned on point, make excellent borders.

Four-Patch Block

Ninepatch Block

Half-Square Triangle Unit

On-point blocks require triangles between them along both sides of the border. The unit size for on-point border blocks and side triangles is the diagonal measurement of the on-point block. To find this figure, multiply the width of the block by 1.41. (Time for the handy calculator.)

For example, suppose you want to put 4" blocks on point around the quilt. Multiply the side measurement of the border block (4") by 1.41 to get the diagonal measurement. Round the number up to the closest usable number (4" x 1.41 = 5.64"; round to 5¾"). This is the unit size and length of the triangles that fill in the border edges. It is also the width of the border.

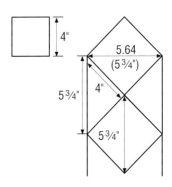

Suppose you have your quilt top done and you want to fit a border to it. Divide the side of the quilt to find the unit size. (See page 20.) Assume that it is 5¾". Divide the unit size by 1.41. Round it down to the closest usable number (5.75" divided by 1.41 = 4.07" or 4"). Make 4" blocks for the border.

Next, cut the triangles to fill the spaces at the border edges. Because the long sides of these triangles will be on the edges of your border, cut them on the straight grain for stability. Cut a square the appropriate size, and then cut twice diagonally.

For example, 4" blocks on point require side triangles with long edges that measure 5¾". Add 1¼". Cut 7" x 7" squares, and then cut the squares twice diagonally into 4 triangles.

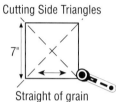

Cutting Side Triangles

Straight of grain

Piece on-point borders in diagonal rows, and then join rows together as shown.

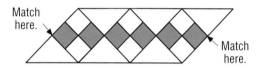

Match here.

Match here.

The side triangles may be larger than necessary if you rounded up when calculating their size. After piecing the border, trim the edges to the necessary ¼"-wide seam allowance beyond the points of the on-point units.

End each border side with two triangles. Trim the excess, being sure to leave a ¼"-wide seam allowance beyond the point of the last on-point block.

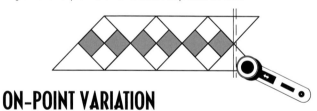

ON-POINT VARIATION

Piece the edge triangles of your on-point border so that a band of color appears to lie behind contrasting on-point border blocks. For other border designs of this type, refer to *Painless Borders* by Sally Schneider, published by That Patchwork Place.

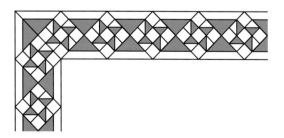

BORDERS MADE OF QUILT-BLOCK ELEMENTS

You may want to use elements from the blocks in the body of your quilt to construct the border. For example, an eight-pointed star has diamonds in its design. Use diamonds in the border to achieve unity. A Jacob's Ladder block has a four-patch unit in its design. Try using a four-patch unit in the border.

Use diamonds from an eight-pointed star design.

Use four-patch units from a Jacob's Ladder design.

Half of a quilt block makes a good border. It repeats the rhythm of the quilt block and extends the size of the quilt without adding a whole block to each side. (See "Ribbon Star with half-block border," page 34.) Use a quarter-block in the corners, or design a simple connecting pattern to flow around the border. (See "Connect the Corners," page 21.)

Whole Block

Half-Block

Quarter-Block

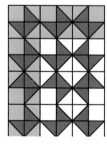

Half-Block Border with Quarter-Block Corner

Half-Block Border with Connecting Corner Design

Two-Unit BORDERS

Combining two identical units creates many design possibilities. Here are a few ideas for designing these interesting borders.

SCALLOPED BORDERS

Simple Scallops

1. Divide the side of the quilt into an even number of units on each side. (See page 20.)
2. Pair two curved units to create a larger curved unit as shown.

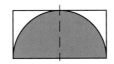

Single Unit   Double Unit

3. Use the pair of units to create a scalloped design.

Overlapping Scallops

1. Complete steps 1 and 2 for "Simple Scallops," above.
2. Draw the border again on tracing paper. Place a single unit at each end as shown.

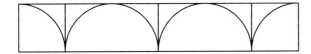

3. Place the tracing-paper border over the scalloped border created in step 3 above. Erase unit lines, if necessary, to create a new overlapping, scalloped border design that you like. (Plan to use different fabrics in the areas that overlap.)

4. Connect the curves at the corners. (See "Connect the Corners," pages 21–22.)

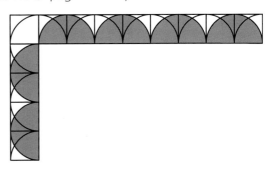

You can piece or appliqué this scalloped border to a plain strip of fabric the same width as the scallops or wider. Or, piece an underlying multistrip border, wider than the scallops so that it shows beyond them. (See "White Tulips," page 30.)

Create appliqué templates using your full-scale border drawing. On paper or template plastic, trace each piece of the design unit. Then prepare appliqué pieces as you would for any other appliqué design.

OVERLAPPING POINTS BORDERS

You can use straight lines to produce the same overlapping effect as shown for the "Overlapping Scallops" border above.

1. Divide the side of the quilt to find the unit size. (See page 20.) You need an even number of units. Use two units to make a pointed design on your graph paper.

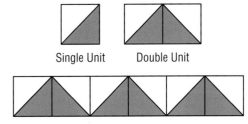

Single Unit   Double Unit

2. Draw another border on tracing paper, exactly like the first one, but turn it upside down.

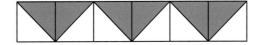

3. Lay one border drawing on top of the other. Erase some lines and use different fabrics in the areas that overlap. Notice that the resulting border is still composed of square units, but there are now two mirror-image units required to make the border.

4. Connect the corners with your starting unit.

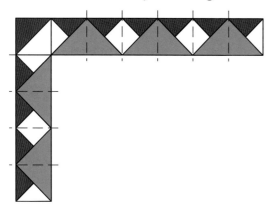

Piecing an Overlapping Points Border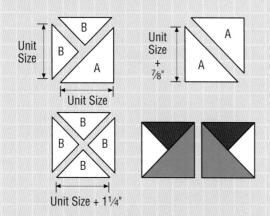

You can piece the Overlapping Points border easily if you begin with square border units. The directions that follow are for the mirror-image units shown in the illustration above.

1. The short side of triangle A equals the unit measurement. Cut squares this size plus ⅞", and then cut *once* diagonally.
2. The long side of triangle B equals the unit measurement. Add 1¼" and cut squares this size. Cut the squares *twice* diagonally.
3. Sew the triangles into mirror-image units and join them to form borders.

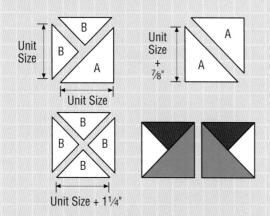

If you overlap rectangular border units to create this design, you create triangles that cannot be cut using the method described above. You must use templates to cut the required shapes.

1. Divide the side of the quilt to find the unit size. (See page 20.) You need an even number of units to alternate diamond colors. The border width is twice the unit size. To design diamond borders on graph paper, draw diagonal lines crossing each border unit from corner to corner.

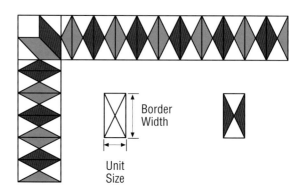

2. Draw a row of units. Erase lines between units. The diamonds appear as you connect the units.
3. Place a half-unit on each end of the border so that the diamonds on each end are complete.

4. Piece the diamond units together in diagonal rows, adding a special unit to each end. The complete unit is made of a diamond (A) and a triangle (B). The special end units require a smaller triangle (C) in addition to A and B. For each side of the quilt you need 2 special end units for a total of 8.

Cutting and Piecing Diamond Borders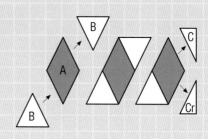

Make paper or plastic templates for pieces A, B, and C, including ¼"-wide seam allowances.

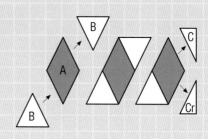

Piece A

1. Cut a 42"-long strip of fabric the width of Template A.
2. Tape the template for piece A to the underside of a rotary ruler. Use it as a guide for cutting diamonds, aligning the template edges with the fabric strip edges. Cut one side of the diamond first, and then turn the ruler around to cut the opposite side.

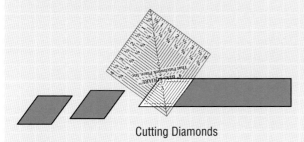

Cutting Diamonds

Piece B

1. On the template, mark the base of the triangle. Measure the distance from the peak of the triangle to the base and cut a strip of fabric that width.
2. Tape the template to the underside of a Bias Square ruler. Use it as a guide for cutting triangles, aligning the base with the fabric edge. Flip the rotary ruler over for every other triangle as you work across the fabric strip.

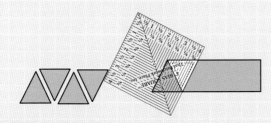

Piece C

Align the template on the corner of the fabric and hold it in place while you position the rotary ruler. Remove the template without disturbing the ruler and cut.

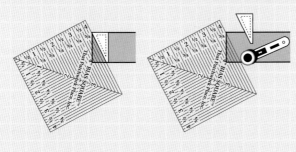

Once you have cut the required number of each piece for your borders, use a sharp pencil to mark the seam intersections on each piece. Then, sew diamond and triangle shapes together to form the borders, as shown, making sure to match seam intersections.

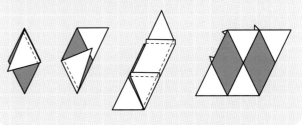

To connect the corners with rhomboids:

1. On graph paper, draw a square the size of the border width. Mark the center of each side of the square and mark the center of the square. Connect the dots. This is a full-size pattern for the corner pieces.
2. Trace the patterns onto paper or template plastic, adding ¼"-wide seam allowances.
3. From fabric, cut 4 of each piece, one for each corner.
4. Use a sharp pencil to mark seam intersections on the squares and rhomboids.

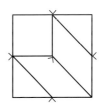

5. Sew the rhomboids (B) together in pairs, being careful to begin the stitching at the marked seam intersection as shown.
6. Add the triangles (C) to the sides of the rhomboids, and then add the square (A), sewing in the direction of the arrows.

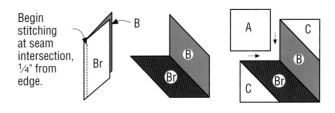

Begin stitching at seam intersection, ¼" from edge.

TWISTED RIBBON BORDERS

Use a dark value and a light value of the same color to create the illusion of a ribbon twisting around the quilt. Diagonally opposite corners match each other in value, two dark, two light.

1. Divide the side of the quilt into an even number of units on each side. (See page 20.) The border width is half of the unit size.

2. Design the unit on graph paper by marking the halfway points of the unit's long sides and drawing diagonal lines from those marks to the opposite corners. Create mirror-image units, as shown. The "ribbon" in one is dark; in the other it is light.

Mirror-Image Units
one light, one dark

3. Sew the units together, alternating light and dark units as shown. Start the border strips for the sides of the quilt with a dark unit and end with a light unit. Start the border strips for the top and bottom of the quilt with a light unit and end with a dark unit. The dark side of the "ribbon" will cross opposite corners of the quilt and the light side of the "ribbon" will cross the other opposite corners.

4. Use plain squares of the background fabric for the corners. Cut them the width of the border plus ½" for seam allowances.

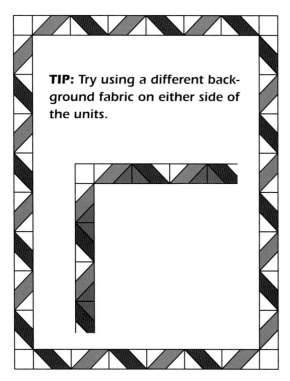

TIP: Try using a different back-ground fabric on either side of the units.

Piecing Twisted Ribbon Border Units

1. Cut rectangles from light and dark ribbon fabrics the unit size plus ½" for seam allowances. For example, if the finished unit measures 2½" x 5", cut rectangles 3" x 5½". Cut half the required number of rectangles from the light fabric and the other half from the dark fabric. For each unit, also cut two squares of background fabric that measure half the unit size plus ½". In the example, cut the squares 3" x 3".

Cut 1 rectangle for each unit (finished unit size + ½").

Cut 2 squares for each unit (half the unit size + ½").

2. Fold the squares in half diagonally with wrong sides together and press lightly. Open the square, place it on one end of a ribbon rectangle, right sides together, and stitch on the pressed diagonal line. Trim the corner to ¼" from the stitching line. Press toward the ribbon fabric. For reversed units, sew the square to the ribbon rectangle with the diagonal seams running in the opposite direction.

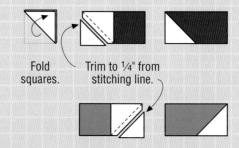

Fold squares.

Trim to ¼" from stitching line.

3. Place another pressed-and-opened square of background fabric on the other end of the ribbon rectangle. Sew, trim, and press as described in step 2.

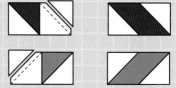

Note: These units are not reversible, so be careful to piece the required number of units slanting left and right using the appropriate values of ribbon fabric in each.

TWISTED RIBBON VARIATION

Create a twisted ribbon border using two different square units. The units in this border change direction at the center point of each side. Use the center unit for a smooth design transition.

1. Divide the side of the quilt into an odd number of square units.
2. To create Unit 1 on graph paper, connect the center point of each side of the square, forming a square inside a square. Use a dark fabric for two opposite corners of the unit and a light fabric for the remaining corners. Use a medium color for the center square.
3. To create Unit 2, connect the center points on only two sides of the square unit. Use dark fabric for the center portion of the block.
4. To create the center unit, repeat the steps for Unit 1, but place the colors so they complete the ribbon as shown.

Unit 1   Unit 2   Center unit

5. Make rows of units, reversing them at the center point, with a center unit in the middle. Start and end each border with Unit 1.
6. Use Unit 2 for corners.

Center
Unit 1 Unit 2 Unit 1 Unit 2 unit Unit 2 Unit 1 Unit 2 Unit 1

Piecing the Twisted Ribbon Border Variation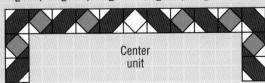

Unit Unit Unit Unit Unit   Unit Unit Unit Unit Unit
2   1   2   1   2   2   1   2   1   2

Center
unit

Unit 1

1. To piece Unit 1 easily, make a full-size drawing of the block. Measure the width of the inner square and add ½" for seam

---

allowances. Cut a 42" strip of fabric that width; crosscut the strip into squares.

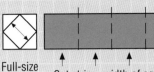

Measure width of inner square.

Full-size block drawing

Cut strip = width of square + ½".

For the corner triangles, cut squares of background and ribbon fabrics that measure one-half the unit size plus ⅞". Cut squares once diagonally to yield two triangles each. Sew triangles to the inner square as shown. If the unit size is 4" square, cut 2⅞" squares (4" x ½ = 2" + ⅞" = 2⅞").

2. Sew triangles to opposite sides of the square, and then add remaining triangles.

Cut squares for corners   Unit 1
½ unit size + ⅞".

Unit 2

1. For the "ribbon," cut a 42"-long strip of dark fabric the width of the unit size plus ½" for seam allowances. Crosscut into squares.
2. Cut squares of light background fabric one-half the unit width plus ½" for seam allowances. Fold squares diagonally and press.
3. Place a background square on one corner of the ribbon square, right sides together, and sew on the diagonal pressing line. Trim away the excess fabric, leaving a ¼"-wide seam allowance. Press toward the dark ribbon fabric.
4. Place another background square on the opposite corner. Stitch, trim, and press.

Cut corner squares
½ unit size + ½".

Cut ribbon squares
the unit size + ½".

Trim to ¼" from stitching.

Center Unit

Piece this unit exactly as you did Unit 1. Only the fabric colors are different.

Appliqué Borders

PLANNING BASICS

Following are methods for making appliqué borders fit your quilts. Appliqué designs are not included. (For appliqué border designs, refer to *Appliqué Borders: An Added Grace* by Jeana Kimball, published by That Patchwork Place.)

Divide appliqué borders into units, just like pieced ones. Mark the units, rather than cutting them out, on a strip of border fabric. Place and stitch the appliqué designs within the marked units.

Divide the Side

Divide the side of the quilt to find the unit size. Use a calculator and graph paper, or try the paper-folding method.

1. From a roll of paper made for calculators or adding machines, cut a piece the exact length of the long side of the quilt top.
2. Fold the paper strip in half. Continue folding until you find a usable unit length. For accuracy, work with only half of the border length and crease the folds sharply. Accordion-fold the creases, rather than folding them over each other. The middle point can be the edge or the center of a unit.
3. Using another piece of adding-machine paper and the same paper-folding technique, find the unit size for the short side of the quilt.

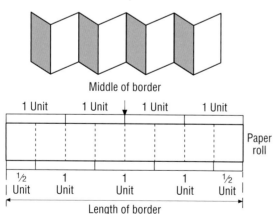

Note: If there is not too much difference between the unit sizes for the sides and top and bottom, they can both be used. If there is a noticeable difference between the unit sizes, consider adding a spacing border to make the sides even. (See "Spacing Borders," pages 23–24.)

Use the Unit

1. Use the paper units to determine the unit size.
2. Determine how wide the border will be.
3. Cut a single border unit from paper. It is helpful to have several of these when experimenting with appliqué designs. Design your appliqué motif within the border unit. Remember that you may have two border unit sizes, one for the short border and one for the long border.

Connect the Corners

Design appliqué corners to flow around the border. If you use a vine, design a loop or a curve in the corner to connect the corner with the border edges.

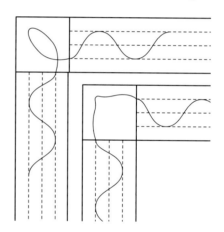

Traditional
APPLIQUÉ BORDERS

VINE BORDERS

A rectangular unit allows for a meandering vine or a swag. Find the unit size and make the border width smaller than the length of the unit.

1. Make a paper unit that fits your quilt and your border width. Fold it into a grid. Fold in half, and then in half again. Open the paper and fold in half from side to side.

2. Draw a gentle curve from one edge to the fold line. Turn the folded unit over and trace the curve onto the other half of it from the fold line to the other edge. The curve will connect at the edge of each unit.

3. Use the curved line to position a bias vine and add leaves or flowers. Or, try extending the curve over two units and use it as a pattern to appliqué a shape with a curved edge to a straight border strip.

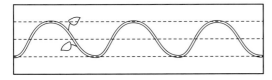

Position a vine.

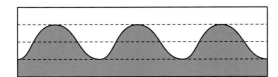

Appliqué a curved edge to a straight background strip.

SWAG BORDERS

1. Create a paper border unit, following the paper-folding technique described in vine borders.
2. Fold your paper border unit in half. On the fold line, mark the depth of the inner and outer edges of your swag.
3. For the inner edge of the swag, draw a gentle curve, starting at the unit corner and touching the fold line at the inner mark.
4. For the outer edge of the swag, start another curve from the unit edge to the outer mark at the fold line. This curve will determine how wide the swag will be at its connection at the unit edge.

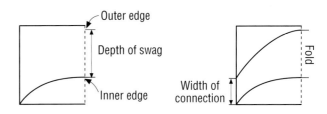

5. Use the same swag depth and connection width for all quilt edges, even if the unit size differs slightly.

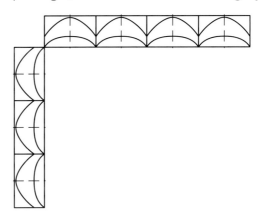

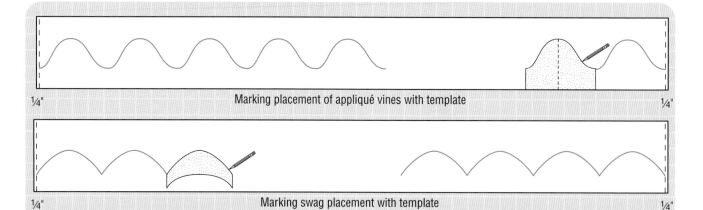

¼"   Marking placement of appliqué vines with template   ¼"

¼"   Marking swag placement with template   ¼"

Making Appliqué Templates for Vine or Swag Borders

1. When you have a paper pattern that you like, use a glue stick to adhere it to a piece of template material (plastic or cardboard). Add a ¼"-wide seam allowance along the straight edge only.

2. Cut out the design, including the seam allowance on the straight edge, and use the curved edge as a drawing guide for the placement of the vine or swag, repeating it over the length of the border.

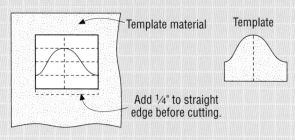

Template material   Template

Add ¼" to straight edge before cutting.

3. Mark the beginning and center of the units in the seam allowance, where it won't show. This helps you to make adjustments later. Start ¼" from one end of the border and mark each repetition, until you are close to the center. Begin ¼" from the other end and mark back toward the center. Make any necessary adjustments before marking the middle repetition. See illustration above.

4. For swag borders, use the template as a placement guide and also as a pattern template. Use a plastic template material that won't wear on the edges. Do not cut the inner curve, but add a ¼"-wide seam allowance to the straight edge as described in step 1, above. Cut the outer curve. Repeat the above process for marking the placement of the outer curves along each border.

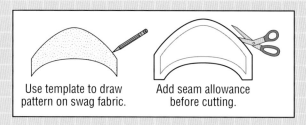

Use template to draw pattern on swag fabric.   Add seam allowance before cutting.

After marking the placement on all borders, cut out the inner curve on the template and use it when drawing the edges of the appliqué swags on the appliqué fabric. Trace the pattern onto the appliqué fabric, leaving plenty of room for seam allowances when cutting out the fabric pieces.

Special
APPLIQUÉ BORDERS

Use an appliquéd sawtooth edge to finish a broad expanse of quilting or a wide appliquéd border. Cut the edge in a plain strip and then slit the strip at the unit measurement. Fold the slit edge under to form points. A sawtooth border requires right angle points. The unit, or base, is twice the height of the point.

A dogtooth border has points that are longer and more pointed than a sawtooth. The height of the point is greater than half of the base, or the unit. It is made using the same techniques as for the Sawtooth Border below.

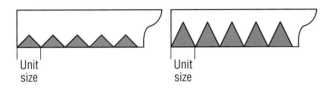

Borders have two sides: interior and exterior. You can appliqué an edge to either one or to both. The corners are handled differently for each type of border.

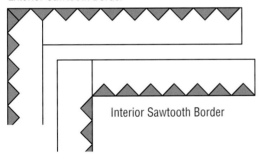

INTERIOR APPLIQUÉD
SAWTOOTH EDGES

(See "White Tulips," page 30.)

1. Divide the side of the quilt to find the unit size. (See page 20.) Add a spacing border to the quilt if needed, so that the unit size is the same on all sides. (See "Spacing Borders," pages 23–24.)
2. Cut two border strips the length of the quilt; cut two strips to equal the width of the quilt.
3. From the fabric for the sawtooth edges, cut four edge strips, the same lengths as the straight borders. Cut the width of the edge strips one-half the unit size plus seam allowances. For example, for 4" units,

you would cut a 2½"-wide strip for the sawtooth border (4" ÷ 2" = 2" + ½" = 2½").

Note: This brings the points to the very edge of the border. If desired, add more space to widen the appliquéd border. Using the example in step 2, if you want to add an extra 1" to the width, you would cut the strips 3½" wide. (4" units ÷ 2" = 2" for points + ½" for seam allowances + 1" added space = 3½".)

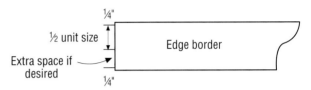

4. Use an erasable chalk pencil to lightly mark a baseline on the right side of the sawtooth fabric where the points will end (¼" from the edge if there is no extra space).

Mark vertical cutting lines at right angles to the baseline. Beginning at the left end, mark ¼" in, and then mark units across the border as shown. There will be an extra ¼" at the other end. Cut on the lines, taking care to stop at the baseline.

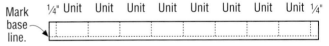

Mark units, beginning and ending ¼" from border edges.

5. Fold under each end at a right angle and press.

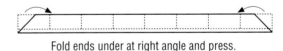

Fold ends under at right angle and press.

6. Machine baste the Sawtooth strip to the background strip, sewing slightly below the marked baseline.
7. Cut on each vertical line, being careful to stop at the marked baseline. Do not cut the basting.
8. At the ironing board, fold under all the cut lines to the baseline and press. Do one direction first, and then go back and do the other direction.

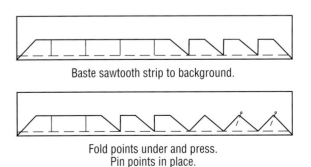

Baste sawtooth strip to background.

Fold points under and press.
Pin points in place.

Baste or pin the points in place. Appliqué by hand or by machine. (Roxi Eppler describes an easy machine-appliqué method in detail in *Smoothstitch Quilts*, published by That Patchwork Place.)

9. Sew borders to the long sides of the quilt.

TIP: If you are planning to quilt in the appliqué border, cut away excess fabric from the back of the appliqué before sewing the borders to the quilt.

10. Apply the remaining two borders in the same way.
11. Cut corner squares to match the border width. Sew corner squares to the border ends and add to the quilt.

EXTERIOR APPLIQUÉD SAWTOOTH BORDERS

1. Cut and sew background fabric strips to all sides of the quilt. (See "Borders with Straight-Cut Corners," page 14.)
2. Divide the side of the quilt. (See page 20.)
3. Cut two appliqué-border strips the same length as the side background borders. Cut two short borders the same length as the width of the quilt, including side borders. To cut the appliqué strips, refer to "Interior Appliquéd Sawtooth Edges," step 2, page 51.
4. Lightly mark with erasable chalk pencil on the right side of the sawtooth fabric as described in "Interior Appliquéd Sawtooth Edges," step 4.
5. Pin a long edge border to the outside edge of each of the long sides of the quilt border. Machine baste on the baseline. Cut slits as in "Interior Appliquéd Sawtooth Edges," step 7.
6. Press points and appliqué as in "Interior Appliquéd Sawtooth Edges," step 8, stopping at last fold. **Important: Do not fold under end segments. Leave them flat.**

Outside edge of quilt border

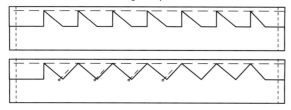

7. Pin the short appliqué strips to the short quilt edges. Fold the ends under at right angles and press over the flat end segments on the long quilt sides to form "mitered" corners.
8. Machine baste on baseline. Cut slits, press points, and appliqué points.

DOGTOOTH APPLIQUÉD BORDERS

Dogtooth edges are similar to sawtooth edges, but they are more pointed. The points are longer than half of the border unit. Add extra width to these appliqué strips for stability.

1. On the right side of the appliqué-border strip, lightly mark a baseline where the dogtooth points will end, ¼" (plus width of extra space for stability) from edge.
2. Fold under ¼" on the opposite edge of the appliqué strip and press firmly.
3. Lightly mark vertical unit lines. At one end, mark ¼" in. From there, measure one unit and mark a vertical line. Continue measuring and marking units along the strip. There will be an extra ¼" at the opposite end.
4. Mark a dot on the folded line, at the center point of each dogtooth unit.

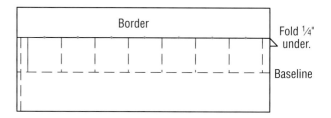

5. Along the baseline, machine baste the appliqué-border strip to the background border.
6. Cut on each marked vertical unit line, taking care to stop at the baseline.

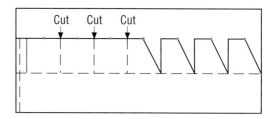

7. Press under from the marked dot to the end of the cut line. Trim away excess fabric, leaving only a ⅛"-wide seam allowance. Press one side of the points, and then the other side.

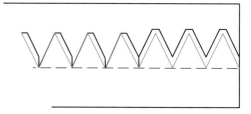

8. Pin or baste points in place. Appliqué folded points to the background border underneath by hand or by machine.

Appliqué Over Piecing

Appliqué works beautifully over a pieced border. (See Patty Kennedy's "Garden Squares," page 29.) Remember to keep the value of the piecing similar and make sure the appliqué pieces contrast enough to show on the pieced border.

QUILTS WITH UNEVEN EDGES

Some quilt patterns end with an uneven edge. Grandmother's Flower Garden, Tumbling Blocks, scalloped, or fan borders are difficult to bind. Consider cutting a wide border and appliquéing the edge of the quilt to that border. (See Martha Peters' "Grandmother's Flower Garden," page 31.) Quilt edges can be needle-turned or pressed under and basted.

1. Measure the quilt length and cut two border strips that length plus a generous extra length. Mark the border at the center and at both ends. (See "Borders with Mitered Corners," page 15.)
2. Working on a flat surface, baste one quilt side to the border, matching centers and end marks. Appliqué the quilt side to the border strip. Repeat with the other side border. Leave about 2" free at each end.

Match centers and ends.

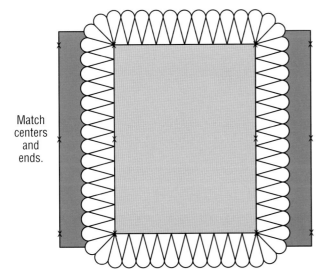

3. Mark top and bottom borders in the same manner. Place the border on the table at right angles and match centers and end marks. Sew or appliqué side borders to the end border, using a square ruler to be certain that the end border forms a right angle with the side borders. Baste and appliqué quilt to the end border. Repeat with the other end border.

Square here.

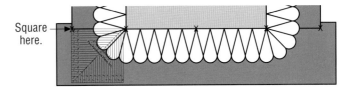

Special Borders

NARROW ACCENTS

When you need just a tiny flash of color, there are two possibilities. Add folded inserts or a very narrow border.

Folded Inserts

1. Cut a 1"-wide strip equaling the length of each quilt side, including seam allowances. If you must piece strips, press seams open to reduce bulk.
2. Fold strips lengthwise, wrong sides together, matching raw edges. Press firmly.
3. Using a ⅛"-wide seam allowance, stitch folded strips to two opposite sides of the quilt.
4. Overlap the corners and stitch the folded strips to the remaining two quilt edges. Now add other borders, using ¼"-wide seam allowances.

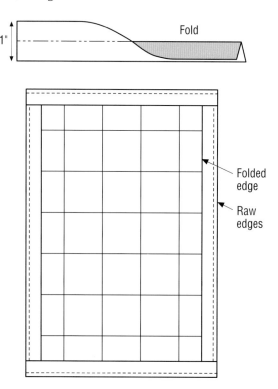

The folded insert is ¼" wide. The fold is not fastened down, creating a three-dimensional effect. Because the fold extends onto the quilt block, it hides pieced points that meet the edge of the block. Use it between straight borders or blocks that have no pieced points at the edges.

Double Folded Inserts

Use a double folded insert to add two color accents to the border.

1. Measure the quilt through the center. From one fabric, cut 1"-wide strips for each side of the quilt. From another fabric, cut 1½"-wide strips. Cut the lengths to match the quilt edges.
2. Fold each strip in half lengthwise, wrong sides together.
3. Layer the two inserts with raw edges together. Stitch to the outside edge of the quilt, using a ⅛"-wide seam allowance. Leave 2" free at each end.

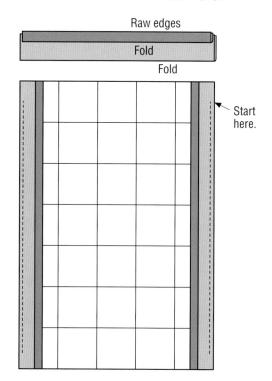

4. Interweave the loose ends on each corner, and then continue as in a single folded insert, at left.

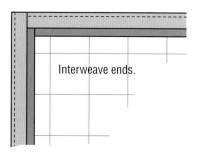

Interweave ends.

Very Narrow Borders

It is easy to rotary cut a straight border; it is not so easy to stitch one without slight variations in width. When the border is very narrow (1" wide or less), any variation is noticeable. Sew the border to the quilt, using an accurate ¼"-wide seam allowance. Before pressing it open, lay the quilt on a flat surface. On the border strip, use a ruler to mark the exact finished size from the seam line you have just stitched. Use the marked line for stitching, not the ¼" guide on your machine.

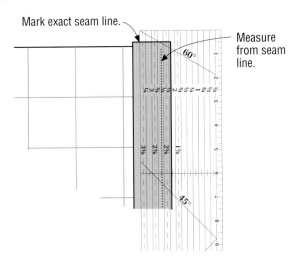

Mark exact seam line.

Measure from seam line.

MEDALLION QUILTS

Medallion quilts build out from a single block or center design with succeeding borders. (See "Edgewise," page 29, and "White Tulips," page 30.) Medallion quilts were popular in early quiltmaking, and they received attention again when Jinny Beyer revived them in the 1980s. Now medallions are appearing in Round Robin quilts. Groups of five or six quiltmakers work together, adding borders to each other's blocks. The most successful medallion quilts have a repeated, unifying factor in each border.

For a simple medallion design, add straight borders of varying widths around a central quilt block. It's a great way to use interesting fabrics and play with contrast and value.

Medallion Quilt

BRACKET BORDERS

"Bracket" the quilt by emphasizing two opposite corners. If the border is pieced, try appliquéd designs. If the border is plain, try a pieced design in two corners. This is a good "formation" for Flying Geese blocks. Find some element that connects the brackets with the rest of the border, ending the corner design with a finished look.

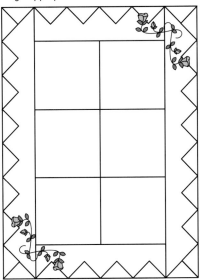

Design appliqué motifs to bracket the corners.

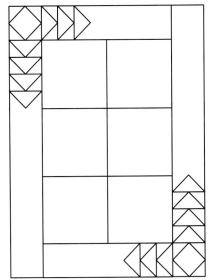

Bracket a border with flying geese.

ASYMMETRICAL BORDERS

The same border doesn't have to go all the way around the quilt. Add borders to only two sides to change a square quilt to a rectangular one. Connect the extra borders to the quilt by framing them or extending a design element from the quilt center, so that they don't appear to be "stuck on" as an afterthought.

To offset the quilt center or to continue a design element, add a wide border to two sides and a narrow one to the other two. (See "Ribbon Star with asymmetrical borders," page 33.)

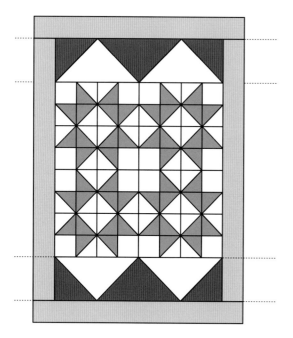

The Final Touch

Now you have the perfect finish on your quilt: beautiful borders. It's ended, right? Not yet. The binding is also an important part of the quilt edge. Integrate the binding with the border by using the same fabric, or frame the quilt one more time by using a contrasting binding. For many binding ideas, refer to *Happy Endings: Finishing the Edges of Your Quilt* by Mimi Dietrich, published by That Patchwork Place.

If your border really is the perfect finish and you don't want to bind it, you can pull the binding all the way to the back of the quilt.

1. Measure the length of the quilt through the middle. Cut two 2¼"-wide binding strips. Fold strips in half lengthwise and press.
2. On the front of the quilt, stitch binding to opposite sides. Use ¼"-wide seam allowances, matching raw edges.

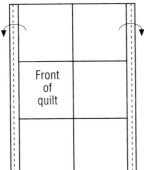

Stitch binding to sides.

3. Trim away as much batting as possible to reduce bulk. Fold the binding outward.
4. Measure the width of the quilt through the middle. Add 4" to that measurement. Cut two 2¼"-wide binding strips to equal the quilt width. Fold strips in half lengthwise and press.
5. Center the binding on the top and bottom quilt edges, leaving 2" at each end. Stitch starting and stopping ¼" from the edge of the quilt. Do not stitch through the side bindings.

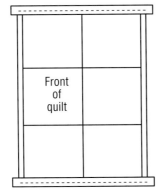

Stitch binding to top and bottom edges.

6. Pull the binding on the side edges to the back of the quilt and pin in place, and then pull and pin the binding on the top and bottom edges.

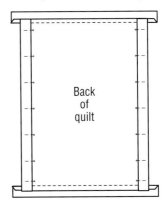

7. Fold under the 2" ends, enclosing the corners. Finger press firmly. Use this fold for the corner, or fold under again, making a mitered corner. Trim as much of the excess bulk as possible.

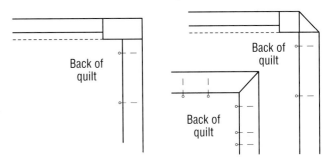

8. Whipstitch the binding to the quilt back.
9. Stabilize the edge. From the back, take invisible running stitches at the very edge, through all the layers except the front. Use matching thread and a long needle, for long stitches.

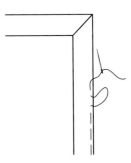

TIP: Rather than fabric binding, you can use 1"-wide woven cotton tape, found in drapery departments. It comes in white only. Add some dye when pre-washing if you want different colors.

RIBBON STAR QUILT PATTERN

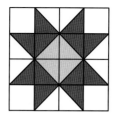

These directions are for 6 blocks, without sashing or borders. You need more fabric for the borders of your choice. Try variations in fabric placement.

Materials: 44"-wide fabric

	8" Blocks	12" Blocks
Light Fabric	⅜ yard	⅝ yard
Medium Fabric	⅛ yard	¼ yard
Dark Fabric	⅜ yard	½ yard

Rotary Cutting

Use your favorite method for cutting half-square triangles, or use these dimensions:

8" Blocks	12" Blocks
From **light** fabric, cut: 4 strips, each 2⅞" x 42"	5 strips, each 3⅞" x 42"
From **medium** fabric, cut: 1 strip, 2⅞" x 42"	2 strips, each 3⅞" x 42"
From **dark** fabric, cut: 3 strips, each 2⅞" x 42"	4 strips, each 3⅞" x 42"

Directions

1. Pair a light and a dark strip, right sides together. For 8" blocks, crosscut strips into twenty-four 2⅞" x 2⅞" squares of each value. For 12" blocks, crosscut strips into twenty-four, 3⅞" x 3⅞" squares of each value. Cut each square once diagonally to yield 48 triangles of each value.

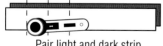

Pair light and dark strip. Crosscut into squares.

Cut squares once diagonally.

2. Sew light and dark triangles together on the diagonal edge and press open. Make 8 of these half-square triangle units for each block (48 total).

3. Pair medium and dark strips, right sides together. For 8" blocks, crosscut strips into twelve 2⅞" x 2⅞" squares. For 12" blocks, crosscut strips into twelve 3⅞" x 3⅞" squares. Cut each square once diagonally.

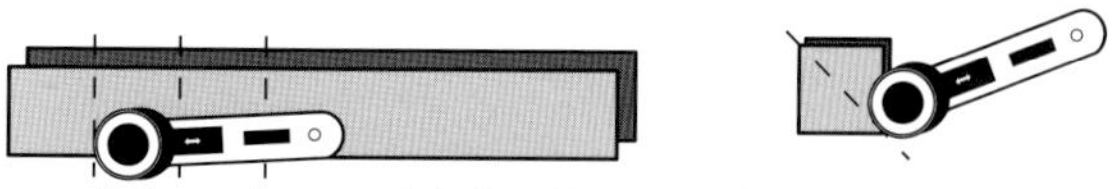

Pair medium and dark strip. Crosscut into squares.

Cut squares once diagonally.

4. Sew triangles together on the long edge and press open. Make 4 units for each block (24 total).

5. From remaining light fabric strips:
For 8" squares, cut 24 corner squares, 2½" x 2½".
For 12" squares, cut 24 corner squares, 3½" x 3½".

6. Assemble blocks.

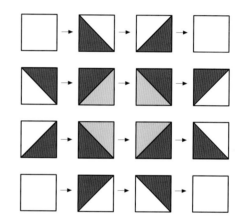

7. Sew them together, and then add a beautiful border.

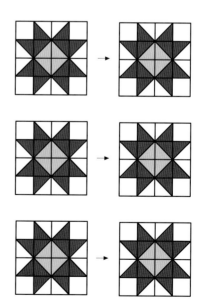

GLOSSARY

Bias—True bias runs at a 45° angle to the straight grain of fabric, but bias can be any angle that is not straight of grain. Stretches easily.

Chain piecing—Sewing many units by feeding them into the sewing machine, one after the other, without backstitching and without lifting the presser foot.

"Divide the Side"—Find the size of a repeated unit for pieced or appliquéd borders.

Grain—Direction of woven threads in fabric.

Lockstitching—Securing the end of a seam that will not be crossed by another seam. Backstitch 2–3 stitches, or take 3–4 stitches in the same spot.

Machine baste—Used to hold a seam in place temporarily. Use the longest stitch on the sewing machine. Loosen sewing machine tension to make stitches easier to remove.

Pin basting—Pinning at right angles to a seam line. Used to hold important matching points or to distribute fullness along a length of border.

Selvages—The tightly woven edges of fabric.

Smoothstitch®—An invisible machine-appliqué technique. Refer to *Smoothstitch Quilts* by Roxi Eppler, published by That Patchwork Place.

Straight grain—Lengthwise grain of fabric (parallel to selvages). Will not give or stretch. Crosswise grain (across the width of the fabric) gives or stretches slightly.

Unit—A repeated design element along the border of a quilt, or the size of that element.

BIBLIOGRAPHY

Beyer, Jinny. *A Quilter's Album of Blocks and Borders.* McLean, Va.: EPM Publications, Inc., 1980.

Dietrich, Mimi. *Happy Endings: Finishing the Edges of Your Quilts.* Bothell, Wash.: That Patchwork Place, 1987.

Eppler, Roxi. *Smoothstitch Quilts.* Bothell, Wash.: That Patchwork Place, 1993.

Hickey, Mary. *Angle Antics.* Bothell, Wash.: That Patchwork Place, 1991.

Hickey, Mary, et al. *Quick & Easy Quiltmaking.* Emmaus, Pa.: Rodale Press, 1993.

Jones, Owen. *The Grammar of Ornament.* Mineola, N.Y.: Dover Publications, 1987.

Kimball, Jeana. *Appliqué Borders: An Added Grace.* Bothell, Wash.: That Patchwork Place, 1991.

Schneider, Sally. *Painless Borders.* Bothell, Wash.: That Patchwork Place, 1992.

ABOUT THE AUTHOR

Paulette Peters discovered quiltmaking on her way through the other needle arts and has been making quilts and teaching quilting ever since. She loves sharing what she has learned with others, especially if it helps them avoid her mistakes. She is a community volunteer, but finds that she is happiest with "needle in hand."

Paulette is a strong supporter of quilt organizations and has served as president of her local guild, Cottonwood Quilters, and the Nebraska State Quilt Guild.

Her quilts have appeared in various exhibits, quilting magazines, and books, including *Rotary Riot*, published by That Patchwork Place. She is the author of *Corners in the Cabin*, also published by That Patchwork Place.

THAT PATCHWORK PLACE TITLES:

AMERICA'S BEST-LOVED QUILT BOOKS®

All-Star Sampler • Roxanne Carter
Appliquilt® for Christmas • Tonee White
Appliquilt® to Go • Tonee White
Around the Block with Judy Hopkins
At Home with Quilts • Nancy J. Martin
Awash with Colour • Judy Turner
Baltimore Bouquets • Mimi Dietrich
Bargello Quilts • Marge Edie
Basic Quiltmaking Techniques for Hand
    Appliqué • Mimi Dietrich
Beyond Charm Quilts
    • Catherine L. McIntee & Tammy L. Porath
Blockbender Quilts • Margaret J. Miller
Block by Block • Beth Donaldson
Borders by Design • Paulette Peters
The Border Workbook • Janet Kime
The Cat's Meow • Janet Kime
Celebrate! with Little Quilts • Alice Berg,
    Mary Ellen Von Holt & Sylvia Johnson
Celebrating the Quilt
Class-Act Quilts
Classic Quilts with Precise Foundation
    Piecing • Tricia Lund & Judy Pollard
Color: The Quilter's Guide • Christine Barnes
Colourwash Quilts • Deirdre Amsden
Crazy but Pieceable • Hollie A. Milne
Crazy Rags • Deborah Brunner
Decorate with Quilts & Collections
    • Nancy J. Martin
Design Essentials: The Quilter's Guide
    • Lorraine Torrence
Design Your Own Quilts • Judy Hopkins
Down the Rotary Road with Judy Hopkins
Dress Daze • Judy Murrah
Dressed by the Best
The Easy Art of Appliqué
    • Mimi Dietrich & Roxi Eppler
Easy Machine Paper Piecing • Carol Doak
Easy Mix & Match Machine Paper
    Piecing • Carol Doak
Easy Paper-Pieced Keepsake Quilts
    • Carol Doak
Easy Paper-Pieced Miniatures
    • Carol Doak
Easy Reversible Vests • Carol Doak
Easy Seasonal Wall Quilts
    • Deborah J. Moffett-Hall
Easy Star Sampler • Roxanne Carter
A Fine Finish • Cody Mazuran
Folk Art Quilts • Sandy Bonsib
Freedom in Design • Mia Rozmyn
From a Quilter's Garden • Gabrielle Swain
Go Wild with Quilts • Margaret Rolfe
Go Wild with Quilts—Again! • Margaret Rolfe
Great Expectations • Karey Bresenhan
    with Alice Kish & Gay E. McFarland
Hand-Dyed Fabric Made Easy
    • Adriene Buffington
Happy Endings • Mimi Dietrich
Honoring the Seasons • Takako Onoyama
Interlacing Borders • Donna Hussain
Jacket Jazz • Judy Murrah
Jacket Jazz Encore • Judy Murrah

The Joy of Quilting
    • Joan Hanson & Mary Hickey
Kids Can Quilt • Barbara J. Eikmeier
Life in the Country with Country Threads
    • Mary Tendall & Connie Tesene
Little Quilts • Alice Berg, Mary Ellen Von Holt &
    Sylvia Johnson
Lively Little Logs • Donna McConnell
Living with Little Quilts • Alice Berg,
    Mary Ellen Von Holt & Sylvia Johnson
The Log Cabin Design Workbook
    • Christal Carter
Lora & Company • Lora Rocke
Loving Stitches • Jeana Kimball
Machine Needlelace and Other
    Embellishment Techniques • Judy Simmons
Machine Quilting Made Easy • Maurine Noble
Machine Quilting with Decorative Threads
    • Maurine Noble & Elizabeth Hendricks
Magic Base Blocks for Unlimited Quilt
    Designs • Patty Barney & Cooky Schock
Make Room for Quilts (revised)
    • Nancy J. Martin
Miniature Baltimore Album Quilts
    • Jenifer Buechel
More Jazz from Judy Murrah
More Quilts for Baby • Ursula Reikes
More Strip-Pieced Watercolor Magic
    • Deanna Spingola
No Big Deal • Deborah L. White
Once upon a Quilt
    • Bonnie Kaster & Virginia Athey
Patchwork Pantry
    • Suzette Halferty & Carol C. Porter
A Perfect Match (revised)
    • Donna Lynn Thomas
Press for Success • Myrna Giesbrecht
Quick-Sew Celebrations
Quilted for Christmas, Book II
Quilted for Christmas, Book III
Quilted for Christmas, Book IV
Quilted Landscapes • Joan Blalock
Quilted Sea Tapestries • Ginny Eckley
A Quilter's Ark • Margaret Rolfe
Quilting Design Sourcebook • Dorothy Osler
Quilting Makes the Quilt • Lee Cleland
Quilting Up a Storm • Lydia Quigley
Quilts: An American Legacy • Mimi Dietrich
Quilts for Baby • Ursula Reikes
Quilts from Nature • Joan Colvin
QuiltSkills • The Quilters' Guild
Quilts Say It Best • Eileen Westfall
Rotary Riot • Judy Hopkins & Nancy J. Martin
Rotary Roundup
    • Judy Hopkins & Nancy J. Martin
Round Robin Quilts
    • Pat Magaret & Donna Slusser
Sensational Settings • Joan Hanson
Sew a Work of Art Inside and Out
    • Charlotte Bird
Shortcuts: A Concise Guide to Rotary
    Cutting • Donna Lynn Thomas
Show Me How to Paper-Piece • Carol Doak
Simply Scrappy Quilts • Nancy J. Martin
Small Talk • Donna Lynn Thomas
Soft Furnishings for Your Home
    • Sharyn Skrabanich
Square Dance • Martha Thompson

Stars in the Garden • Piece O'Cake Designs
Start with Squares • Martha Thompson
Strip-Pieced Watercolor Magic
    • Deanna Spingola
Stripples • Donna Lynn Thomas
Stripples Strikes Again! • Donna Lynn Thomas
Strips That Sizzle • Margaret J. Miller
Sunbonnet Sue All Through the Year
    • Sue Linker
Surprising Designs from Traditional Quilt
    Blocks • Carol M. Fure
Threadplay with Libby Lehman • Libby Lehman
The Total Bedroom • Donna Babylon
Traditional Quilts with Painless Borders
    • Sally Schneider & Barbara J. Eikmeier
Tropical Punch • Marilyn Dorwart
True Style • Peggy True
Two-Color Quilts • Nancy J. Martin
The Ultimate Book of Quilt Labels
    • Margo J. Clabo
Variations in Chenille • Nannette Holmberg
Victorian Elegance • Lezette Thomason
Watercolor Impressions
    • Pat Magaret & Donna Slusser
Watercolor Quilts
    • Pat Magaret & Donna Slusser
Weave It! Quilt It! Wear It!
    • Mary Anne Caplinger
Welcome to the North Pole
    • Piece O' Cake Designs
Whimsies & Whynots • Mary Lou Weidman
WOW! Wool-on-Wool Folk Art Quilts
    • Janet Carija Brandt
Your First Quilt Book (or it should be!)
    • Carol Doak

FIBER STUDIO PRESS TITLES:

The Art of Handmade Paper and
    Collage • Cheryl Stevenson
Complex Cloth • Jane Dunnewold
Dyes & Paints • Elin Noble
Erika Carter: Personal Imagery
    in Art Quilts • Erika Carter
Fine Art Quilts: Work by Artists of the
    Contemporary QuiltArt
    Association
Inspiration Odyssey • Diana Swim Wessel
The Nature of Design • Joan Colvin
Thread Magic • Ellen Anne Eddy
Velda Newman: A Painter's Approach
    to Quilt Design • Velda Newman with
    Christine Barnes

FIBER STUDIO PRESS

PASTIME TITLES:

Hand-Stitched Samplers
from I Done My Best
    • Saundra White
The Home Decorator's Stamping Book
    • Linda Barker
A Passion for Ribbonry • Camela Nitschke

Many titles are available at your local quilt shop. For more information, write for a free color catalog to Martingale & Company, PO Box 118, Bothell, WA 98041-0118 USA.

☎ U.S. and Canada, call **1-800-426-3126** for the name and location of the quilt shop nearest you.
Int'l: 1-425-483-3313   Fax: 1-425-486-7596
E-mail: info@patchwork.com
Web: www.patchwork.com

6.98